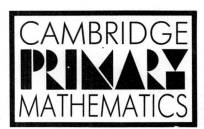

CAMBRIDGE
PRIMARY
MATHEMATICS

Module 7

Teacher's resource book

*Roy Edwards, Mary Edwards
and Alan Ward*

CAMBRIDGE
UNIVERSITY PRESS

Published by the Press Syndicate of the University of Cambridge
The Pitt Building, Trumpington Street, Cambridge CB2 1RP
40 West 20th Street, New York, NY 10011-4211, USA
10 Stamford Road, Oakleigh, Melbourne 3166, Australia

First published 1991
Third printing 1993

Printed in Great Britain by Scotprint Ltd., Musselburgh

British Library cataloguing in publication data

Edwards, Roy 1931–
Cambridge primary mathematics
Module 7
Teacher's resource book
1. Mathematics
I. Title   II. Edwards, Mary 1936–
III. Ward, Alan 1932–
510

ISBN 0 521 35829 9

The authors and publishers would like to thank the many schools and individuals
who have commented on draft material for this course. In particular, they would
like to thank Ronalyn Hargreaves (Hyndburn Ethnic Minority Support Service),
John Hyland, Norma Pearce and Anita Straker, who wrote the chapter on 'Using
the computer'.

VN

CONTENTS

Mathematical content of chapters in Module 7

BOOK 1

Money
Multiplication of money
Mini-enterprise projects

Shape 1
Rotational symmetry

Number 1
Multiplication of ThHTU by 1 digit
Division of ThHTU by 1 digit
Linking multiplication and division
Rounding and rounding errors on the calculator

Length
Scale and scale drawings

Area
Area of composite shapes using cm^2

Volume
Finding volumes by counting cubes
Calculating volumes in cm^3

Probability 1
Using the probability scale from 0 to 1
Estimating probabilities

Map reading
Finding location by means of grid references
Using Ordnance Survey maps

Data 1
Using decision tree diagrams

Percentages
Using simple percentages

BOOK 2

Number 2
Revision of multiplication and division by 1 digit
Multiplication of 2 digits by 2 digits
Multiplication of 3 digits by 2 digits

Number 3
Negative numbers

Data 2
Revision of graphical work
Designing and using data collection sheets
Pie charts, scatter graphs

Probability 2
Revision of likelihood of events and possible outcomes
Using the probability scale from 0 to 1
Estimating probabilities
Notation for probability ($\frac{1}{n}$)

Angles 1
Revision of language of angles
Measuring of angles to 5°
Congruence
Angle properties associated with intersecting and parallel lines
Bearings

Measurement 1
Revision of scale
Unitary ratios
Height finding

Number 4
Revision of decimal notation in the context of measurement
Decimals and decimal places

Co-ordinates
Revision of co-ordinates in the first quadrant
Co-ordinates in all four quadrants

Data 3
Revision of line graphs
Conversion graphs
Two-way tables

Number 5
Revision of fractions
Addition and subtraction of fractions
Using percentages
Converting fractions to percentages
Calculating fractions and percentages of quantities

Number 6
Using simple formulae and equations
Expressing simple functions symbolically

Angles 2
Revision of line properties
Measuring angles to 1°
Constructing 2–D shapes
Identifying equal angles
Investigating tessellations

Number 7
Revision of place value and rounding
Index notation
Trial and improvement methods
Approximation, using significant figures
Generating sequences

Measurement 2
Revision of measurement and estimation
Imperial units and their metric equivalents

Number 8
Revision of division
Division of 3 digits by 2 digits

Shape 2
Revision of symmetry
Investigating centres, axes and planes of symmetry

Number 9
Revision of number patterns
Square and triangular numbers
Prime, square, cube, square root, cube root, multiples, factors

Time and shape
Revision of 24 hour clock
Time zones
Networks and traversability

INTRODUCTION

Aims

Cambridge Primary Mathematics is designed for 4–11 year old children. It takes into account current thinking in mathematical education and in particular it provides opportunities for:

- exposition
- discussion
- practical work
- consolidation and practice
- problem-solving
- investigational work

It is also designed to make mathematics relevant for the children and there is considerable emphasis on presenting the mathematics in real situations. Calculator work is incorporated throughout at the discretion of the teacher and ideas are given for using the computer. The materials are for children of all abilities and particular thought has been given to those with special education needs.

Cambridge Primary Mathematics provides you with a sound foundation for all your mathematics teaching. It is *not* trying to take the place of a teacher, but rather acknowledge your professionalism. All the materials that make up Cambridge Primary Mathematics are giving you, the teacher, a core of valuable resources, so you can teach mathematics in whatever way suits you best. Cambridge Primary Mathematics can be used in its entirety and does not need additional material in order to provide a thorough mathematics curriculum. However you may prefer to teach using a variety of materials and Cambridge Primary Mathematics will give you a rich source of teaching ideas which you can supplement.

The materials

Each topic can be introduced to a class or group with activities and discussion. Ideas for these are given in the teaching notes. The children can then try the relevant chapter in the pupils' book.

Pupils' books

Each chapter in pupils' book 1 has its concepts developed in three stages.

Section A is intended for all children and care has been taken to make it easily accessible. It consolidates the introduction, discussion and practical work provided by the teacher and finishes with a

Module	For teachers	Pupils' core materials	Reinforcement and enrichment	Assessment
1 4–5 yrs	Module 1 Teacher's resource pack	Module 1 Workbooks	Module 1 Games pack Module 1 Extra cut-up cards and rules Module 1 Rhymes pack	
2 5–6 yrs	Module 2 Teacher's resource pack	Module 2 Workcards	Module 2 Games pack Module 2 Extra cut-up cards and rules	
3 6–7 yrs	Module 3 Teacher's resource pack	Module 3 Workcards	Module 3 Games pack Module 3 Extra cut-up cards and rules	
4 7–8 yrs	Module 4 Teacher's resource book	Module 4 Book 1 Module 4 Book 2 Module 4 Answer book	Module 4 Games pack Module 4 Puzzle pack Module 4 Skill support activities Module 4 Extension activities	Module 4 Review sheets
5 8–9 yrs	Module 5 Teacher's resource book	Module 5 Book 1 Module 5 Book 2 Module 5 Answer book	Module 5 Games pack Module 5 Puzzle pack Module 5 Skill support activities Module 5 Extension activities	Module 5 Review sheets
6 9–10 yrs	Module 6 Teacher's resource book	Module 6 Book 1 Module 6 Book 2 Module 6 Answer book	Module 6 Games pack Module 6 Puzzle pack Module 6 Skill support activities Module 6 Extension activities	Module 6 Review sheets
7 10–11 yrs	Module 7 Teacher's resource book	Module 7 Book 1 Module 7 Book 2 Module 7 Answer book	Module 7 Games pack Module 7 Puzzle pack Module 7 Skill support activities Module 7 Extension activities	Module 7 Review sheets

problem or investigation. Children who need further reinforcement can be given work from the skill support masters.

Section B is suitable for the majority of children and covers the same concepts in more breadth, and again includes an investigation.

Section C, which includes a further investigation, can be used as extension work. Children with a special interest or aptitude for mathematics can explore topics in greater depth with the *Extension Activities.*

Module 7 Book 2 differs from the other books; children do not follow the normal pattern in working through sections A, B and C.

Section A revises and consolidates the concepts covered up to, and including, Level 4 of the National Curriculum. Some children may only attempt this section.

Sections B and C cover the attainment targets in level 5 and many of those in level 6. It is not necessary for children working on sections B and C to complete section A first, unless the teacher requires it for revision purposes.

The work in these sections is usually based on a theme of interest to children (e.g. school magazine, birds, etc.) in order to give the material more cohesion and to make it relevant to the environment.

This structure ensures that all children can follow a basic course of mathematics, covering all the concepts at whatever stage is appropriate to them. Organisationally this allows the teacher to teach the children as a class or in groups, as all sections cover the same topics but at increasing breadth. Children who complete only section A will not be left behind in the progression. The A, B, C format will provide for problem-solving and investigational skills to be developed across all areas of the mathematics curriculum by all children.

Logos

Throughout the pupils' books, certain logos are used to show children the items they will need or which would be particularly helpful.

 shows that squared paper is needed.   indicates that a calculator would be useful.

 means a clock face stamp would be useful.   shows that glue is required.

 tells children they can time themselves.   indicates that scissors are needed.

The logos are used partly to reduce the language in instructions and partly to give children visual clues for items they need.

Coloured text

Two colours of text are used in the pupils' books in order to help the children. Black text is used for instructions and information. Blue text shows the parts the children will need to record in their books.

Answer books

For Modules 6 and 7 the answer books contain simple lists of answers.

Games packs

There is a games pack for each module. The games are linked to the mathematical content of the course and are intended to consolidate children's skills and also to encourage children in logical thinking and development of strategies.

Puzzle packs

There is a puzzle pack for each of Modules 4–7. These packs provide extra extension material and additional interest.

Skill support activities

The worksheet masters, at least one for each chapter, provide fresh approaches and reinforcement for those children who need it.

Extension activities

These topic based activities are challenging, and will extend the conceptual understanding of the more able children.

Organisation and management

The materials needed are readily available, but to help you further there is a complete list of all equipment required at the end of this book. Materials can be collected, boxed and labelled so that they are easily accessible to the children.

Cambridge Primary Mathematics is not intended as a scheme for children to work at individually, but instead to give you control over how the mathematics is taught. The following ideas have been suggested by teachers who used the early materials.

- Introduce each topic using your own ideas plus the information in the teacher's notes.
- Let children develop the concepts at their own levels using the A, B, C structure and the skill support masters.
- Some of the investigations are particularly suitable for work and discussion in a large group or whole class.
- Overcome a shortage of equipment, like balance scales, by organising groups to work at several different activities.
- Use the games and puzzles to reinforce particular teaching points or skills as part of the normal mathematics lesson.
- Look for the calculator games in the teacher's notes.

Cambridge Primary Mathematics gives you the space to include your own ideas and to develop concepts as part of the whole curriculum.

Using the teacher's resource book

There is a section in the teacher's book for each chapter of the pupils' material. The format for each one is as follows:

Purpose

This outlines the mathematical objectives of the pupils' pages for the particular chapter.

Materials

This lists all the materials required by the pupils as they work through the mathematics.

Vocabulary

This provides you with the essential mathematical vocabulary that is used in the pupils' books. You will know which words the children will be meeting and be able to introduce them during earlier teaching sessions.

Teaching points

This section contains possible teaching approaches and activities for all the mathematics in the pupils' books. Many of these are introductory activities for the concepts. As well as activities, the notes are full of ideas and games to add to your own approach and already successful methods. You will also find ideas for mental skills, such as a quick way to add 2-figure numbers, that will help children master and enjoy mathematics.

The Cockcroft report emphasises the importance of discussion between teacher and child, and between children. These notes give you suggestions for questions to set discussion going, and give children the opportunity to talk, ask questions and develop their mathematics. It also allows you to listen to the children and see how their understanding is developing.

There are also ideas for introducing the practical activities and further suggestions for developing these.

Using the calculator

In this part there are ideas for incorporating a calculator into mathematics. The calculator is to be used at your discretion and there will be occasions when you won't want the children to use one. However, you will probably want to have calculators readily available and there will be times when children will need a calculator to help them complete their work. The calculator is a useful aid for children to develop a particular piece of mathematics. In the pupils' book a logo is used to indicate where a calculator will be especially useful.

Links with the environment

These notes show how the mathematical ideas may be related to the everyday environment or linked to other curriculum areas. You can develop these ideas further and incorporate them into topic work across the curriculum.

Notes on investigations

Investigations are essentially open-ended situations where different approaches can be made. The notes are not meant to be used rigidly but to give guidance and suggestions for developing the mathematics. Investigations are discussed in more detail on pages 10–11.

ISSUES IN MATHEMATICS TEACHING ▮

Language in mathematics

Language gives mathematics context and meaning. It sets the scene, poses problems and gives information. But the way language is used and how children interpret it is crucial to their success and progress. How then does language affect mathematics?

The words used are important. Some are found only in mathematics and have to be learned, like 'parallelogram' and 'right-angle'. Some, like 'add' and 'equal', have the same meaning in or out of mathematics, and some, the ones most likely to cause problems, have different meanings according to their context; 'table' and 'difference' have both mathematical and ordinary English meanings.

Not only are the words important but so is the style of writing. There will be *explanations* of concepts, methods, vocabulary, notation and rules. *Instructions* will tell the reader what to do, and *exercises* will give practice of the skills and set problems or investigations. *Peripheral text* will introduce exercises or give clues to ways of approach, and *signals* give structure to the text with headings, letters, numbers, boxes and logos. Children must be able to see their way through all these forms of writing.

But, in addition to the words and writing, mathematics also involves reading visual information. A good mathematics text should use illustrations effectively to add information. They should not be purely for decoration, or related but not essential to the mathematics. There are also many forms of visual language which children need to understand. These include tables, graphs, diagrams, plans and maps. It is important to teach children to decode this information, interpret and make use of it, and present their answers or conclusions in different forms.

The skills children need for reading mathematics have only been touched on here. An awareness of the complexities involved will help you to overcome any difficulties caused by language and so prevent them becoming mathematical problems too. Useful books to read are *Children Reading Mathematics*, by Hilary Shuard and Andrew Rothery (John Murray) and *Maths Talk*, from The Mathematical Association.

Mathematics and special needs

Many difficulties which children experience with mathematics are not genuinely mathematical. Children with special educational needs, for whatever reasons, may have problems with mathematics because of a wide variety of factors. By looking at possible causes of difficulty many problems can be prevented or at least significantly helped.

In writing Cambridge Primary Mathematics careful attention has been given to making the mathematics accessible to *all* children, particularly in the A sections. The following areas have been looked at carefully.

Mathematical language

- Familiar words
- Words in context
- Repetition of important words and phrases
- Clear and unambiguous instructions
- Clear indication of response expected
- Sentences of a suitable length and structure
- Clear and unambiguous symbols

Presentation

- Appropriate quantity of work
- Interesting and relevant illustrations
- Variety of presentation
- Attractive page layout to encourage a positive attitude

Independence

- Clear indication of apparatus needed
- Materials that will be readily available
- Instructions children will be able to read and understand

Recording

- No unnecessary writing
- Minimum writing to help children with motor-control difficulties
- Word prompts to aid spelling

Practical work

- Plenty of practical activities
- Use of concrete apparatus encouraged
- Practical work encouraged and built in with the maths

Attitude

- Children are given a purpose to their work
- The mathematics is put in meaningful contexts
- Mathematics is related to other curriculum areas

There are some aspects of special needs that can only be dealt with by you in the classroom. For example, children may not be able to get all the equipment they need and so labelling boxes and drawers with pictures can help. Sometimes their handwriting can cause problems through poor letter or number formation, or because they are left-handed, and extra practice in this may be needed.

Skill support masters for section A give extra support and reinforcement for those children needing further practice or consolidation. Where possible, alternative methods of approach have been given but the masters are essentially to strengthen work already done.

Mathematical language, presentation, independence, recording, practical work and, just as important, the attitude children bring to their work are all vital for success. By identifying whether a difficulty is genuinely mathematical you can remove or alleviate many problems. You know your children best, and by looking at all the factors affecting their learning you can meet their special needs. By doing so, you can give them the love and fascination for mathematics so that they achieve to the best of their potential.

English as a second language in mathematics

Research suggests that many children lack a firm grasp of the language of mathematics. In the case of children with English as a second language, this is often compounded by other language difficulties.

All pupils need the opportunity to hear and use the correct mathematical vocabulary. They need to develop concepts and the appropriate language together. You should not assume that because children can perform a mechanical mathematical task that they understand the associated language. You can check this by discussion with the pupil.

Practical activities are the essential starting point for any topic. Every opportunity should be taken to use correct mathematical vocabulary with pupils and to encourage them to use it when talking with other children and teachers. Where possible this vocabulary should be reinforced in other curricular areas, e.g. art and craft, games, PE etc.

Activities which offer opportunities for group work are also very useful for language development since the children are required to cooperate and to discuss the work they are doing. Investigations, calculator and computer work all lend themselves to pair or group activities.

When discussing work or activities with the children you should try to avoid the questioning approach which only requires short or one-word answers. Instead encourage full explanations of pupils' thoughts and actions using the correct vocabulary.

Weaknesses in mathematical language and the comprehension of mathematical texts often only become apparent in the junior school where greater emphasis is placed on reading and recording. Even pupils who can read a mathematical text may well be unable to interpret it. Oral discussion, individually or in groups, will help to develop the skills required.

Special attention should be given to words which sound similar; for example, 'hundred' 'hundredth', and 'seventeen' 'seventy'. Pronunciation is often a problem with second-language learners because certain sounds may not exist in their mother tongue. However, they should be encouraged to attempt to make the distinctions clear.

Words which have a mathematical meaning different from that in normal English – like 'similar', 'difference' and 'table' – also need special attention.

It is important not to skimp on the language aspect of mathematics in order to 'push on' with mechanical exercises and recording. A weak language base will lead to downfalls later.

Mathematics and gender

There is evidence that in the past many girls have under-achieved in mathematics. The reasons for this are complex and only an indication can be given here. Although the problem may only become apparent in the secondary school, the roots of it can often lie in the primary school.

In Cambridge Primary Mathematics there has been an attempt to produce material which will encourage girls as much as boys. As far as is possible, the pupil materials show equal numbers of girls and boys, show them participating equally in all types of activity, and illustrate how mathematics can be used in situations familiar to girls as well as to boys.

However, the written materials are only a part of the mathematics teaching. There is a great deal that you, as a teacher, can do to help the girls in your class.

- Try to encourage girls to use apparatus and toys which encourage spatial awareness, for example, Lego. Girls often have less access to this kind of toy at home, and an intuitive feeling for space is important for later work.
- Try to make sure that you spend as much time interacting with girls as with boys. It is very easy to give more time to a group of demanding boys and to leave a group of quiet girls to get on with their work.
- There has been research which shows that girls in primary schools are less likely than boys to have a calculator, to own a digital watch and to have a microcomputer at home. You may find it useful to do a survey of your class so that you are aware of the children who may need extra help with these items.

If you would like to find out more about encouraging girls to achieve their potential in mathematics, then you may find it useful to read *Girls into Mathematics* by the Open University (published by Cambridge University Press). The book was written mainly for teachers in secondary school, but many of the activities could be adapted easily for use in primary schools.

Using the calculator

Calculators are now widely available and are used extensively in the world of work. It is therefore important that children should learn to use them intelligently. The course has been written on the assumption that children have calculators available, although the extent to which they are used is left to the individual teacher.

In the pupils' books a logo is used to show activities which would particularly benefit from the use of a calculator. The teaching notes contain suggestions to develop use of the calculator including many ideas for games.

A basic school calculator is all that is required. Ideally these should be to hand whenever children are doing mathematics and it should be natural for children to turn to them when they are needed. Children with special needs may need to use a calculator to complete section A even in places where the logo is not shown.

The use of the calculator has brought about a shift in the content of the mathematics included in the course. There is less emphasis on straight computation and more on problem-solving. It is also important that children develop mental strategies so that they can check that calculator answers are approximately correct and they have not miskeyed. Ideas for developing these mental skills are given in the teaching notes.

Using the computer

The computer is a useful tool for developing mathematical ideas. It can also be a useful way to get children to discuss their mathematics.

Make the most of any opportunities you have for using the computer during mathematics. Children should work at it in twos or threes as this allows scope for discussion. It is important that within each group, there is no one child dominating and restricting the participation of the others. For this reason it may be necessary to select the groups carefully.

Ideas for using the computer with Module 7 are given in the chapter on using the computer on pages 12–31. This chapter was written by Anita Straker who has a lot of experience in this area. The ideas are not restricted to any particular model of computer.

There is an information handling package planned for use alongside the course.

Investigations

Investigations are essentially open-ended activities where children may devise various approaches. They provide an ideal opportunity for children to devise their own pieces of mathematics, to use logical reasoning, and to discuss mathematics between themselves.

Ideally children should work on investigations in small groups. This gives them the chance to talk, think and express their ideas.

When they have worked on an investigation as a group for a while, it can be very beneficial to have the group report to the rest of the class on how they approached the task. This gives an opportunity for the class to see alternative approaches and various problem-solving techniques.

It is important not to make remarks that judge children's contributions and not to become so involved that the investigation ceases to be the child's. The ideal contribution from the teacher is questions such as:

> 'Why did this work?'
> 'Will it work with other shapes or numbers?'
> 'What would happen if . . .?'

The teaching notes include comments on the investigations. These are not meant to be used rigidly but merely to give some indication of where the investigation might lead. Other approaches may be just as good, or better! Children should be encouraged to find their own way of recording and to ask further questions in order to extend their work.

Algorithms

Algorithms are methods for doing calculations. On the whole, these detailed methods are not given in the texts in order to allow freedom of choice. You can introduce your preferred method, or alternatively the children can devise their own. If children do work out their own algorithms then a teaching approach similar to investigations can be used with children sharing their ideas. This approach has the advantage that the method becomes the child's own and they are more likely to remember it.

Use of practical work

Children should be encouraged to use apparatus and concrete materials whenever possible. It is important that children have plenty of experience in practical situations before moving on to doing more abstract activities. They should not be hurried into making this step.

The materials required for this course are widely available. A checklist of what you will need for Module 7 is given at the end of the book.

USING THE COMPUTER ███████████████

The computer's contribution to children's mathematical work comes through using:

- specific programs in which children can explore mathematical ideas
- adventure games and simulation which support mathematics across the curriculum
- software tools like databases and programming languages which support open-ended problem-solving

In each case, the software can act as a stimulus to children to talk about mathematical ideas. Through their informal discussion with each other and with their teacher children can build sound intuitive ideas about mathematical concepts. Children need to work in small groups at the computer, so that they have a chance to share and to talk about what is happening on the screen.

Specific programs

Although there are many 'drill and practice' mathematics programs, there seems little point in using the computer for practice when there is already an abundance of mathematics practice material in books, on workcards and on worksheets.

Some of the most attractive of the specific programs are in the form of strategic games or puzzles. In these the children need to focus on the strategy which is to be used, and they will often use mental skills in the process. It is important that teachers link the use of these programs to the children's work away from the keyboard: both preliminary and follow-up activities need to be planned in advance.

There are also specific programs which encourage mathematical investigation. The starting point of the investigation should be through practical work away from the computer, but when the diagrams become too complicated, or the calculations too difficult, the computer program can take over.

Adventure games and simulations

Adventure games, based on fantasy, and simulations, based on fact, give children opportunities to solve problems across the curriculum in a context of fact or fantasy. Simulations like *Cars – Maths in Motion* (Cambridge Software House), *Suburban Fox* (Newman College) or *Bike Ride* (Energy Pack, Cambridge University Press) require strategic thinking and planning, and the use of a range of mathematical and other skills. Adventure games, like *The Lost Frog* (ESM), *Dread Dragon Droom* (RESOURCE), *Puff* or *Martello* (A. Straker), all have a series of mathematical puzzles and problems which need to be resolved.

Primary children often lack confidence in problem-solving situations but such programs can provide them with additional opportunities for developing their mathematical thinking and increasing their range of problem-solving strategies. The role of the teacher in encouraging discussion about the possible forms of solution is an important one here. Questions like 'What would happen if instead . . .?', or 'How many different ways could we . . .?', or 'Would it be possible to . . .?', all help to extend the children's thinking about a particular problem.

Databases

Databases support a range of statistical work across the curriculum. Databases can be used to encourage the children to ask questions, to collect, organise and analyse data, and to find patterns and relationships.

There are two kinds of databases which are useful.

Sorting Game (MESU), *Seek* (Longman) and *Branch* (MEP Project Work Pack) are databases based upon a branching-tree structure. They encourage the use of very precise mathematical description in sorting and classifying. Children can set up binary-tree classification systems, using the program alongside the practical sorting activities which take place throughout the primary school.

Databases like *Our Facts* (MESU) or *Factfile* (CUP) work in the same way as a card index system. Graph drawing packages like *Picfile* (CUP), which display the data graphically, are very helpful here.

Programming

Young children begin 'to program' as soon as they start to find ways of recording things like a sequence of moves in a game, the commands to give to a battery-driven robot, or the shapes which are needed to make up a picture. A computer program, like a sheet of music or a knitting pattern, is simply a set of precise, coded instructions arranged in an appropriate order, and programming is another way in which children can use the computer as a tool to explore mathematical ideas.

The programming language which is most often used in primary schools is Logo. The point of introducing young children to programming with Logo is to allow them to feel in control, to give them a way of clarifying their ideas, and to encourage them to order their thoughts logically. Although the children will need to be taught some simple programming techniques, the emphasis needs to be not on learning these techniques, but on the mathematics that can be explored through programming.

Number (National Curriculum AT2)

Number notation, estimation, approximation

Work on place value is still important at this stage, focusing especially on large numbers and decimal fractions. Activities with concrete materials like an abacus or Dienes blocks, and activities with calculators, can be supplemented by the use of place-value games in the form of computer programs. After they have used the computer it is important that children discuss or write about the strategies which they used. Ask them 'How did you know where to place your marker?' or 'Were there any quick ways of winning?'

- *Place Value Activities* (ESM): a set of six different place-value games.
- *BoxeD* (MicroSMILE): compete against the computer to put ten decimal numbers in boxes in the right order.
- *GuessD* (MicroSMILE): guess a number with up to three decimal places using clues of 'too big' or 'too small'.
- *Minimax* (MicroSMILE): put five numbers in boxes, do a sum, and make a smaller or bigger number than the computer.
- *Zoom* (Teaching with a Micro 2): zoom in and out on a number line refining the degree of accuracy with which a number's position can be described.

There are many different computer games and puzzles which help children to develop strategies for ordering common fractions.

- *Bango* (Mathematics 9–13): burst a balloon by identifying the point at which it is tied as a fraction of the distance along a line.
- *Hunt* (Mathematics 9–13): guess a common fraction between 0 and 1.
- *Wall* (MicroSMILE): a fraction wall appears and the bars slide out – the users must reassemble the wall.
- *Tower* (MicroSMILE): add bricks to towers of fractions.

Number operations

Other computer games help the children to develop and practise mental strategies.

- *Number Games* (ESM): a set of ten different number games.
- *Number Games for Nimbus* (Capital Media): a set of games and other activities requiring the use of mental arithmetic.
- *Taxi, Adds up to, Darts* (MicroSMILE): number games involving logic and strategy help one or two players to reinforce addition and subtraction skills.

A good follow-up activity to the use of strategic number games and puzzles on the computer is to suggest that the children make changes either to the numbers or to the rules and devise their own game or puzzle using A4 card, dice, or other apparatus.

The activities which children have been doing with their calculators can also be done with a computer. By programming the computer, using either Logo or BASIC, the children can explore the effects of typing in some simple statements to see the result on the screen. Using the PRINT command, the children can try to solve some problems. For example,

- Which pairs of whole numbers give the result of 0.1 when one of the numbers is divided by the other? Which pairs of decimal numbers? What about 0.01?
- 5814 is the product of three consecutive numbers. What are they?
- $1\bullet2 \times 14\bullet = 24\bullet40$. What are the values of the missing digits?
- What number, when multiplied by itself, gives the answer 2?

A simple program written in BBC BASIC, available for the Nimbus as well as for Acorn computers, can be used to find the average (mean) of a set of numbers.

```
10    PRINT "How many numbers? ";
20    INPUT N
30    PRINT "Enter each number. Press RETURN after each
      one."
40    TOTAL = 0
50    FOR T = 1 TO N
60        INPUT T
70        TOTAL = TOTAL + T
80    NEXT T
90    PRINT "THE AVERAGE IS "
100   PRINT TOTAL / N
110   END
```

This program can be used to investigate problems like:

- Find four numbers with an average (mean) of 32.
- Find five numbers with an average of 3.2.

The PRINT command is also useful for investigating the relationship between pairs of numbers which result from a practical experiment. For example, the circumference and diameter of a number of different sized objects like jam jar or pan lids or cake tins, and larger objects like hoops or quoits, can be measured to produce a table of results:

Circumference (cm)	Diameter (cm)
9·5	3
14	4·5
63	20

By typing in the first number of the pair divided by the other:

```
PRINT 9.5 / 3
PRINT 14 / 4.5
PRINT 63 / 20
```

and so on, the children are helped to an understanding of the underlying relationship and will reach an approximation for π: for example, 'the circumference divided by the diameter is always a little bit more than 3'.

A quicker way, using Logo, would be to use the procedure:

```
TO FIND :circumference :diameter
    PRINT [The circumference divided by the diameter is]
    PRINT :circumference / :diameter
END
```

All that is then needed is to type FIND 9.6 3, or FIND 63 20.

For many children, one of the most exciting ways of using the computer is participating in an adventure game or simulation in which different mathematical puzzles or problems will need to be solved. Adventure games and simulations offer opportunities for cross-curricular work, since they stimulate many different activities away from the keyboard. Programs like these are best used by small groups, so that discussion about strategies can take place. The children will need to keep careful records of their positions, the routes followed and the decisions made.

Some adventure games which provide a series of situations in which number skills and strategic thinking are both developed are:

- *Martello Tower* (ESM): the object is to find your way through a tower and out to sea again solving many puzzles and problems as you do so.
- *Titanic* (ESM): investigate the sinking of the Titanic.
- *Cars − Maths in Motion* (Cambridgeshire Software): a simulation of a car race on a choice of tracks.
- *Let's Explore London* (Cambridgeshire Software): decide where to go in London. Each visit involves using some mathematics.

Algebra (National Curriculum AT3)

Number patterns

The use of computer software to support number work can provide opportunities to explore number patterns. Although discovery of a pattern is a first step, children need to be encouraged to do more than this. Patterns can help to identify or to explain relationships, to make predictions or to form generalisations. The programs require the children first to spot a pattern, and then to make use of it in some way. By making generalisations about the patterns which they see, or about the relationships which they discover, and putting these into words, the children start to use algebraic ideas.

It is important to start investigations like these away from the computer using pencil and paper or other apparatus. Encourage the children to predict what will happen before they try something out. Help them to organise in a sensible way the results which they gather and to look for patterns which might help them. When diagrams become too difficult to draw, or when the numbers become too difficult to calculate, move to the computer program. At the end of the investigation, ask the children to tell you in their own words what they have found out.

- *Monty* (Slimwam 2): the python called Monty wriggles around on a number grid. The challenge is to discover which numbers he is covering.
- *Counter* (Slimwam 2): set a starting number, and a jump size, so that patterns of digits can be explored.
- *Patterns 1* (MEP Primary Mathematics Pack – RESOURCE): choose the width of a grid and investigate the patterns created by one or two multiples.
- *Going Down, Triangles, Routes, Pascal* (Mathematics 9–13): various mathematical investigations.
- *Multiple, Factor, Rose, Spirals, Nim* (MicroSMILE): various mathematical investigations.

Programs like *Counter* and *Patterns 1* are open ended – small tools which carry out particular tasks. It is up to the users to decide what they would like to do with them. For this reason, it is best if a teacher works with the children at the computer, helping them to select and to refine suitable ideas.

For example, with *Counter* you could decide to start on 559, and jump back in 24s.

- What is the pattern in the sequence of the units digits? In the sequence of tens digits?
- How many digits are there in the tens digits pattern? Can you explain this?
- Stop when you get to 7. What will happen next? Why?

With *Patterns 1*, you could make a pattern of 11s on a grid with seven columns.

- Would 198 be in the pattern? How do you know?
- What number would be at the top of the column with 157 in it?
- What other grids produce the same pattern for multiples of 11? What do all these grids have in common?
- What would the pattern of 11s look like for a grid with five columns? Can you explain why?

The programming language BASIC could be used to print out the first few multiples of 11.

```
10    FOR NUMBER = 1 TO 10
20    PRINT NUMBER * 11
30    NEXT NUMBER
40    END
```

This program can be modified to investigate the outcome of multiplying a number of any size by 11. By retyping line 10 so that it reads, for example,

10   FOR NUMBER = 50 TO 65

blocks of numbers can be printed out and examined for patterns to help determine a rule. The program can easily be changed to print, for example, sequences of square numbers or cubic numbers.

Logo procedures can be used to investigate possible rules. For example, a procedure called, say, TRY that has a variable input can be written and hidden away so it works like a function machine:

```
TO TRY :number
    PRINT 25 * :number + 1
END
```

By typing TRY 5, TRY 2, TRY −3, and so on, a selection of outputs can be generated. Players can use these to help them guess the rule 'hidden' in the machine. Encourage the children to try small negative numbers as inputs, as well as positive numbers, and also to try zero as an input. When the rule has been discovered and tested, the middle line of the procedure can be replaced by a similar line so that the next group of children have a different rule to investigate.

Number patterns can also be investigated using a spreadsheet, if one is available. The advantage of the spreadsheet is that tables of data and different sorts of graphs can also be printed out to aid the investigation or to help communicate what has been discovered. Some introductory spreadsheets which include a range of graphs and charts are:

- *PSS* (Cambridgeshire Software): a spreadsheet for the Nimbus specially written for primary school users.
- *Grasshopper* (Newman College): an introductory spreadsheet for the BBC or Nimbus.

Co-ordinates, graphical representation of functions

There are a number of computer programs which require the children to make use of co-ordinates as part of a game or puzzle. Some of these programs are computerised versions of well-known board games such as three-dimensional noughts and crosses or Othello. In the computer versions the players need to use co-ordinates in order to tell the computer where they want to place a marker.

- *Co-ordinate Jigsaw* (Maths with a Story 1): create a jigsaw by specifying the co-ordinates of the puzzle pieces to be changed over.
- *Pirate Gold* (Maths with a Story 2): the aim is to fill a treasure chest with gold by hunting for it on an island or under the sea.

- *Rhino* (MicroSMILE): hunt a lost rhinoceros on a 10 × 10 co-ordinate grid making use of clues which give the distances along the grid lines.
- *Locate* (MicroSMILE): a small cross appears within a large blank square. The object is to locate the cross by typing in two numbers to represent co-ordinates.

It is also possible for children to produce line drawings based on co-ordinates by programming the computer in either Logo or BASIC. In Logo, the command to move the turtle to position (X, Y) on the screen is

SETPOS [X Y]

If the pen is up, the turtle will move to the position (X, Y) without drawing a line. If the pen is down, the turtle draws a line as it moves. The mid-point of the screen is the position (0, 0). Try experimenting with the SETPOS command, first with the pen up and then with the pen down. The command CS will clear the screen and either HOME or SETPOS [0 0] will put the turtle back in the centre. If you are not sure about the position of the turtle on the screen, they typing

PRINT POS

will produce the co-ordinate position for you.
  This Logo procedure will draw a triangle.

```
TO  TRIANGLE
    PENUP
    SETPOS [300 − 100]
    PENDOWN
    SETPOS [− 50 250]
    SETPOS [− 200 − 250]
    SETPOS [300 − 100]
    PENUP
END
```

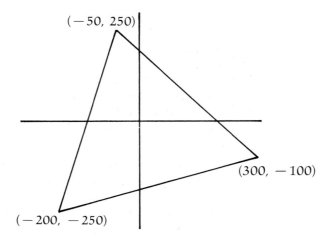

One game that children enjoy programming for each other starts by one group secretly drawing a small square somewhere on the screen. The turtle is then returned to the centre position. The next group then tries to move the turtle into the square by using the smallest number of SETPOS commands.

Similar ideas can be developed using BASIC although the position (0, 0) is generally the bottom left-hand corner of the screen. Before you begin you must make sure that the screen is ready for drawing. You can do this by typing MODE 1. This command will clear the screen and place the 'pen' in the bottom left-hand corner.

There are then two commands which are useful to use. The command

MOVE 100, 300

makes the 'pen' move to the co-ordinate position (100, 300) without drawing a line, whereas the command

DRAW 300, 500

draws a straight line from the existing position to the new position of (300, 500).

Children could try this BASIC program to draw a square.

```
10    Mode 1
20    MOVE 100, 200
30    DRAW − 300, 200
40    DRAW − 300, − 200
50    DRAW 100, − 200
60    DRAW 100, 200
70    END
```

Once the program has been run and is working in a satisfactory way, some decoration could be added to the square by adding further lines. For example, try drawing the diagonals. Try drawing a smaller square inside the bigger square with its corners on the diagonals.

Whether they are programming in Logo or in BASIC to make pictures or patterns using co-ordinates, encourage the children to suggest their own ideas for drawing. Provide them with squared paper on which to make their plans before they go to work at the computer.

The first graphs of functions which children draw will probably be to do with plotting the co-ordinates of, say, the three times table and joining the points. This is simply a representation of the graph $y = 3x$. Alternatively, they may plot a graph showing distance and time: for example, to plot the distance travelled by a car going at a constant 30 mph.

Two programs which can help children to interpret graphs, and to draw similar graphs to represent 'stories' for friends to read and interpret, are these.

• *Eureka* (MEP Microprimer): a dynamic graph of the level of water as a man takes a bath, puts the taps on or off, the plug in or out, and so on.

- *Bottles, Traffic* (Teaching with a Micro 2): more dynamic graphs, showing water in bottles of various shapes, or the speed of traffic.

Shape and space (National Curriculum AT4)

Properties of 2D and 3D shapes

Computer software can provide opportunities for building shapes and patterns and talking about them.

- *Take Half* (MicroSMILE): different dissections of a square into two halves.
- *Build* (Slimwam 2): construct three-dimensional images made from frameworks of cubes.
- *Maths Talk* (MEP Primary Maths): generate shapes and patterns and use them as talking points.

Software can also be used to help discovering the relationships which allow shapes to fit together to cover a surface in a tessellating pattern.

- *Picture Craft* (BBC Soft): patterns can be built up using different colours, shapes, and movements, then printed out.
- *Tiles* (MicroSMILE): the screen displays a 10×7 array of square tiles. The tiles may be rotated through $90°$ individually, or in lines (horizontal, vertical, diagonal) to make interesting patterns.
- *Mosaic* (Advisory Unit): generate tiling patterns by creating a motif which is then transformed in various ways.
- *Tilekit* (Slimwam 2): formulate rules for generating patterns to cover a surface using one or more different shapes.

Using programs like these the children could try to fill the screen with:

- L shapes
- T shapes
- squares of two different sizes
- squares within squares
- combinations of squares and oblongs
- other shapes of their own choosing

The children can also try these same challenges using Logo, first drawing the shape of their tile and then trying to repeat it to fill the screen.

It is important to discuss with the children the properties of shapes which fit together without leaving any spaces. Why will four squares fit together round a point? Why do certain patterns create an effect of straight lines?

Angle, direction, symmetry, enlargement

Children who have been accustomed to working with Logo should have a firm grasp of angle as a measure of turn. They will be comfortable with the use of degrees as a unit of measurement. They will be aware that a right-angled turn of 90 is needed to make the corner of a square and will have used commands like RIGHT 180 or LEFT 180 to make the turtle turn to face the opposite direction.

Words like 'acute', 'obtuse' and 'reflex' can be introduced as children discuss their Logo drawings. 'Here the turtle turned LEFT 135 so it turned through an obtuse angle. Where else did you make the turtle turn through an obtuse angle? Here it turned RIGHT 60. If it had turned LEFT instead, what reflex angle would you have used?'

Logo can be used, for example, to investigate the angles in stars with different numbers of points.

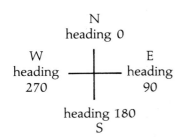

You can also use Logo to give children a feel for compass bearings using the command SETH, to set the turtle's heading: that is, the direction in which it is pointing. A heading of 0 is straight up the screen, a heading of 90 is to the right, 180 is straight down, and 270 is to the left.

Try typing this sequence of commands.

SETH 90 FD 50 SETH 135 FD 50 SETH 90 FD 50

The children can try tracing a path by using compass bearings and will enjoy planning 'walks' for the turtle in this way. Alternatively, they can use a computer game which requires them to use angles, bearings or compass directions.

- *Angle 360* (MicroSMILE): estimate the size of angles drawn on the screen.
- *Merlin's Castle* (ESM): avoid Merlin the Wizard and his traps as you explore the surroundings of a grassy bank using compass directions.
- *Snooker, Pilot, Goldhunt, Maze* (MicroSMILE): programs using angles or directions. In *Goldhunt*, the north line is unlikely to point to the top of the map!
- *Mapping Skills* (ESM): seven related programs locating treasure using co-ordinates, compass directions and scale to calculate distances.

In their work on line or rotational symmetry, children can try to make symmetrical pictures or patterns with the same tiling programs that they have used to investigate space filling with simple tessellations. Other programs which can be helpful are:

- *Turnflex* (Maths with a Story 2): this is a puzzle in which the aim is to rebuild a picture using mirrors and rotations.
- *Symmetry Patterns* (Maths with a Story 1): this program allows children to create patterns using different kinds of symmetry, with one, two or four mirror lines.
- *Reflect* (MicroSMILE): try drawing the reflection of a pattern generated on the screen.

Line symmetry can also be investigated using Logo. For example, this procedure will draw a zigzag of lines on the right-hand side of the screen.

```
TO ZIGZAG
    FD 100
    RT 90
    FD 250
    RT 90
    FD 400
    RT 90
    FD 100
END
```

What procedure would draw the reflection of the zigzag in a vertical line down the centre of the screen? In a horizontal line across the screen?

Rotational symmetry can be investigated with Logo by seeing what would be required to produce patterns like these.

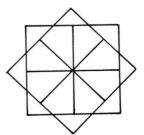 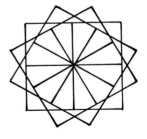

Logo is useful for developing ideas of scale to enlarge or reduce a shape. For example, what modifications would need to be made to the ZIGZAG procedure to produce a similar shape one tenth of the size? Many children find it surprising that all angles remain the same while linear distances are all reduced (or enlarged) by the same factor. Any procedure which children have written to produce a simple pattern or picture can be modified in the same manner. It is often an interesting struggle for them to discover the modifications which can be made to a procedure similar to this one for drawing a circle in order to produce one which is relatively larger or smaller.

```
TO CIRCLE
    REPEAT 36 [FD 5 RT 10]
END
```

Children who are familiar with variables will have used procedures similar to this one for drawing a pentagon. By varying the number used for the input they can explore the effects of changing the scale factor to produce pentagons of various sizes.

```
TO PENTAGON :size
    REPEAT 5 [FD :size RT 72]
END
```

Work on scale developed through Logo can be complemented by practical work with construction kits, microscopes, maps, aerial photographs, and so on, and supplemented by work with other computer programs: for example,

- *Tile Stretch* (Maths with a Story 2): players take turns to fit square tiles on a board. Tiles can be stretched by a factor of 1, 2 or 3 along either the length or the width of the tile.

Data handling (National Curriculum AT5)

Record, process, represent, interpret data

The computer is capable of storing data and producing a wide variety of graphs, charts and tables very quickly and accurately. It makes it possible for children to spend time on the important skills of handling real information collected by themselves. For a particular problem or investigation, these skills involve:

- deciding what data to collect
- deciding how to collect it
- deciding how to record or represent it
- framing questions, and using the data to find answers
- explaining results
- communicating findings

There is an easy-to-use program which is still useful at this stage to display and print the data which children have collected.

- *Datashow* (Information Handling Pack from MESU): a group of children, or a teacher working with them, can enter up to eight items of data, sort the items either numerically or alphabetically, and display the data in a table, bar chart or pie chart.

The program is most suitable for displaying counts of various kinds, perhaps made by a whole class, or even the whole school. The data can often be collected very quickly on a 'hands up who . . .' basis. It can be used to represent the results of a simple survey or scientific work: for example,

Wind direction	Number of days in July
N	●
NE	● ●
E	● ● ●
SE	● ● ● ●
S	● ● ● ● ● ● ● ●
SW	● ● ● ● ● ●
W	● ● ●
NW	●

Another way of using the computer to handle and display information is by using a database.

- *Our Facts* (MESU – Information Handling Pack): an introductory database which is extremely easy to use. It displays information in tables, on Venn diagrams, in pictograms, block graphs, pie charts and scatter graphs. Depending on the data being collected, it can handle about 60–80 records.
- *Grass* (Newman College): a more sophisticated database which can handle much larger amounts of information. It displays information in pie charts and count graphs.

A database can support any cross-curricular work in which children are gathering and using information. For example, if children as part of a science project are making a study of the shapes of different parachutes then they might want to examine connections between the radius of the canopy, the material used for the canopy, the number of strings, the length of the strings, the weight in the cup, and the time taken to descend a fixed height (preferably several metres on a still day). The record for each parachute might look like this.

PARACHUTE: a code number to identify the parachute
MAKER: name of person who made it
CANOPY: radius of canopy in centimetres
MATERIAL: material used (e.g. polythene, cotton, net)
STRINGS: number of strings
LENGTH: length of strings in centimetres
WEIGHT: weight placed in cup in grams
TIME: time for descent in seconds

The outcomes of their investigations should enable the children to answer questions like: 'What would you do if you wanted to make a parachute which descends more slowly? What were the average dimensions of the parachutes that came down quickly? What is the maximum weight which should be used in a parachute with a canopy of radius 15 centimetres?'

When the children are making interpretations from the graphs and charts which they produce, encourage them to use familiar fractions to make estimates of proportions. When examining pie charts, for example, it is relatively easy to see things like 'about three quarters of the parachutes can down in less than four seconds' or 'about one third of the parachutes had eight strings'. Ask them to suggest reasons for their findings. For example: Why does polythene make a slow parachute? Why is a weight needed?

Children who are confident with BASIC programming might make their own simple database. The data for five people is listed in lines 50 to 90, and gives the person's name, age, height, weight, leg length, time to swim 25 metres and time to run 50 metres. More data can be added between lines 50 and 100, as long as the number of people in line 10 is amended.

```
10     FOR person = 1 TO 5
20     READ name$, age, height, weight, leg, swimtime,
       runtime
30     IF height > 135 THEN PRINT name$
40     NEXT person
50     DATA Tanya,10,130,31,52,13,10
60     DATA Ali,11,132,32,52,15,9
70     DATA Sam,10,136,35,55,14,14
80     DATA Karen,11,135,30,54,18,12
90     DATA Disa,11,136,32,56,16,14
100    END
```

By changing line 40, different enquiries can be made. For example,

```
30     IF height > 135 AND runtime < 15 THEN PRINT
name$
```

The best known decision tree program to classify and identify a collection of objects is *Animal*, included in the Microcomputer Pack for each school. This allows children to frame questions in order to identify animals. More flexible programs allow questions to be framed about any set of the children's choice.

- *Sorting Game* (Information Handling Pack from MESU): large text makes the display easy to read by a group of children; records of questions and objects are kept separately for children to refer to.
- *Branch* (Information Handling Pack from MESU): the graphic display of the 'tree' helps children to appreciate that framing questions which divide the sets of objects into two equal halves enables a single object to be identified in the shortest possible time.

Branching tree programs are always best used when they are based upon the children's direct experience, first-hand research and/or practical work. They can be used to classify, represent and identify properties of objects in many areas of the curriculum: for example, science: sweets, rocks, metal objects, clothes, fabrics, pond life . . .

mathematics: shapes, numbers, coins or stamps, directions to reach local landmarks . . .

language: characters in a story, library books . . .

history: gravestones, architectural features, old packets and tins, battles . . .

geography: holiday regions, railway routes, fruits from overseas, wine labels . . .

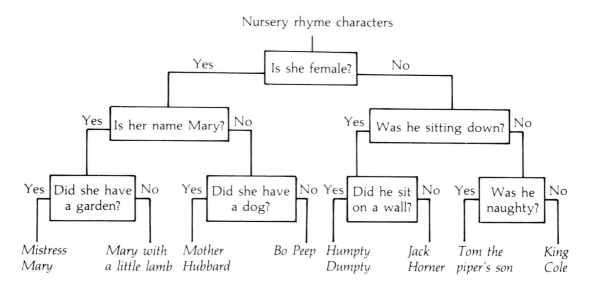

Nursery rhyme characters

Probability

The program *Datashow* can also be used to collect guesses or predictions and then checked with the real result to see how the predicted and actual results compare with each other. Some suggestions are:

Way I will come to school tomorrow:
walk, bus, train, tube, bike, car.

I think I can swim:
10 metres, 20 metres, 100 metres, more.

Tomorrow's wind direction will be:
N, NE, E, SE, S, SW, W, NW.

I think I can run 50 metres in:
10–12 seconds, 13–15 seconds, 16–18 seconds, . . .

In 60 rolls of a dice, I think the number of 6s will be:
0–10, 11–20, 21–30, 31–40, 41–50, 51–60.

After each display using *Datashow*, it is important to ask the children 'What does the graph show us or tell us?' and 'Why do you think that?' Ask them to place outcomes or events in order of 'likeliness' and to talk about the 'chance' of something happening. Encourage them to use words like 'unlikely', 'possible', 'likely', 'highly likely', 'highly probable' and to associate these words on a scale from 'impossible' to 'certain'.

Some other programs which simulate experiments with dice or coins, and which can help children to appreciate simple ideas of probability are:

- *Dice Squares* (Maths with a Story 2): roll dice and predict outcomes.
- *Roller* (Mathematics 9–13): roll a dice to accumulate a score but all is lost if you roll a one.
- *Dicecoin* (Slimwam 1): simulates throwing dice and tossing coins – useful for gathering lots of data quickly.
- *Digame* (Slimwam 2): strategic games using dice.
- *Predict, Pinball* (MicroSMILE): predict outcomes of rolling dice, tossing coins, or rolling balls on a pinball table.

NATIONAL CURRICULUM SOFTWARE LINKS

AT2: Number

Number and number notation, estimation and approximation

Matching, Number Snap, Cubes, Beads 1 and *2* (Getting Ready for Maths)
Lift Off with Numbers, Playing with Places, Ordering (Shiva)
Boxes 1–4, Counting Words, Find Me (Place Value Activities, Number Games for Nimbus)
Sizegame (MEP Primary Maths)
Ergo (Microprimer)
Monty, Counter (Slimwam 2)
Boxes, Guess, GuessD, Tower (MicroSMILE: The First 31)
Minimax, Jumping, Boxed, Wall (MicroSMILE: The Next 17)
Tenners, Magnify (MicroSMILE: 11 More)
Bango (Mathematics 9–13)
Hunt (Mathematics 9–13, Number Games for Nimbus)
Zoom (Teaching with a Micro 2)
Lineout (Teaching with a Micro 4)

Number operations

Additional Fun, Happy Times, Shares for All, 4 rules OK? (Shiva)
Line up, Spots, Make 37, Make 57, Chains, Counters, Play Train (Number Games from ESM, Number Games for Nimbus)
Toyshop, Teashop (MEP Primary Maths, Number Games for Nimbus)
Two Dice Race Game (Maths with a Story 1)
Taxi, Adds up to, Darts (MicroSMILE: The Next 17)
Magic (MicroSMILE: 11 More)
Criss Cross, Remainders, Links (Mathematics 9–13)
Conceal, Target, Flags, Gusinter (Number Games from Capital Media, Number Games for Nimbus)
Going Down (Mathematics 9–13, Number Games for Nimbus)
Cars, Titanic
Logo, BASIC

AT3: Algebra

Patterns, relationships, sequences, generalisations

Cubes, Beads 1 and *2* (Getting Ready for Maths)
Differences (Shiva)
Spots, Ask Me (Number Games from ESM,
Number Games for Nimbus)
Ergo (Microprimer)
Monty, Counter, Spiro (Slimwam 2)
*Tales, Dots, Lines, Polygon, Bounce, Diagonal,
Clocks, Squares, Crosses* (Mathematical
Investigations from Capital Media,
Mathematical Investigations for Nimbus)
Patterns 1 and *2, Eggs* (MEP Primary Maths
Pack, Mathematical Investigations for Nimbus)
Multiple, Factor, Rose, Spirals, Nim
(MicroSMILE: The First 31)
Define, Identify, Hopslide, Quilts, Tadpoles
(MicroSMILE: The Next 17)
Numbers, Magic (MicroSMILE: 11 More)
Going Down, Triangles, Routes, Pascal
(Mathematics 9–13, Mathematical
Investigations for the Nimbus)
Takes and Adders (Teaching with a Micro 4)
Number (Teaching with a Micro 5)
Puff, Martello Tower, L
Grasshopper, PSS
Logo, BASIC

*Co-ordinates, graphical representation of algebraic
functions*

Shape Hunt (Place value) or *Search* (Number
Games for Nimbus)
Co-ordinate Jigsaw (Maths with a Story 1)
Pirate Gold (Maths with a Story 2)
Plod (Teaching with a Micro 1)
Ghosts (Teaching with a Micro 4)
Elephant, Rhino, Locate (MicroSMILE: The First
31)
Lineover (MicroSMILE: The Next 17)
3 in a Line, Foxes, Regions (MicroSMILE: 11
More)
Eureka (Microprimer)
Bottles, Traffic, Sunflower (Teaching with a
Micro 2)
Circles, Squares (Mathematics 9–13,
Mathematical Investigations for Nimbus)
Grasshopper, PSS
Logo, BASIC

AT4: Shape and space

Properties of 2D and 3D shapes

Paintpot
Shape Hunt (Place value) or *Search* (Number
Games for Nimbus)
3 in a Line (MicroSMILE: 11 More)
Tiling
Maths Talk (MEP Primary Maths Pack,
Number Games for Nimbus)
Picture Craft
Factory
Take Half, Build (MicroSMILE: The First 31)
3D Maze (MicroSMILE: The Next 17)
Logo

*Location, direction, angle, symmetry, enlargement,
translation, networks*

Treasure Hunt (MEP Infant Pack)
Maze (Slimwam 2)
Crash, Spanish Main, Watchtower (Microprimer)
Picture Craft
Symmetry Patterns, Colouring Puzzle (Maths with
a Story 1)
Turnflex, Tile Stretch (Maths with a Story 2)
Tiling
Tilekit (Slimwam 2)
Factory
Bounce (Mathematical Investigations)
*Take Half, Reflect, Snooker, Angle 90, Goldhunt,
Pilot, Maze* (MicroSMILE: The First 31)
Angle 360, Newtiles (MicroSMILE: The Next
17)
Alice, Mirror (MicroSMILE: 11 More)
Mosaic
Frieze
Kaleidoscope
*Lost Frog, Puff, Martello Tower, L, Merlin's
Castle, Let's Explore London, Titanic*
Logo

AT5: Handling data

Collect, record, process, represent and interpret data

Launching Logic, Sets, Decisions (Shiva)
Sorting Game
Branch
IDelta
Data Show (Information handling pack,
Number Games for Nimbus)
Our Facts
Grass
Grasshopper, PSS
Quest
Eureka (Microprimer)
Bottles, Traffic, Sunflower (Teaching with a
Micro 2)
Times (Teaching with a Micro 4)

Estimation and calculation of probability

Boxes 4 (Place value, Number Games for
Nimbus)
Dice Squares (Maths with a Story 2)
Predict (MicroSMILE: The First 31)
Minimax (MicroSMILE: The Next 17)
Roller (Mathematics 9–13, Number Games for
Nimbus)
Digame (Slimwam 2)
Routes, Pascal (Mathematics 9–13,
Mathematical Investigations for Nimbus)
Pinball (MicroSMILE: 11 More)
Logo, BASIC

Addresses of suppliers

Advisory Unit for Microtechnology
Endymion Road
Hatfield
Hertfordshire AL10 8AU

ATM
Association of Teachers of Mathematics
7 Shaftesbury Street
Derby DE3 8YB

BBC Soft
BBC Enterprises
80 Wood Lane
London W12 0TT

Cambridgeshire Software House
The Town Hall
St Ives
Huntingdon
Cambridgeshire PE17 4AL

Capital Media Software
is available from ILECC (see below)

ESM
Duke Street
Wisbech
Cambridgeshire PE13 2AE

ILECC
Educational Computing Centre
John Ruskin Street
London SE5 0PQ

Logotron Ltd
Dales Brewery
Gwydir Street
Cambridge CB1 2LJ

MUSE
Microcomputer Users in Education
PO Box 43
Houghton on the Hill
Leicestershire LE7 9GX

NCET
National Council for Educational Technology
Sir William Lyons Road
Science Park
University of Warwick
Coventry CV4 7EZ

Newman College Computer Centre
Genners Lane
Bartley Green
Birmingham B3T 3NT

Northampton Computer Education Centre
Teachers' Centre
Barry Road
Northampton NN1 5JS

Research Machines Ltd
Mill Street
Oxford OX2 0BW

Shell Centre for Mathematical Education
University of Nottingham
Nottingham NG7 2RD

Notes

Many local authorities have licensing arrangements for software so it is worth contacting your
LEA adviser before making any purchase.

MEP Primary Project Packs: The MEP Infant Pack and the MEP Primary Mathematic Pack are
available free through lcoal education authorities.

Name of program	BBC version	Nimbus version
Databases and spreadsheets		
Grass	Newman College	Newman College
Grasshopper	Newman College	Newman College
PSS: primary spreadsheet	Cambridgeshire Software	Cambridgeshire Software
Quest	Advisory Unit	Advisory Unit
IDelta	. . .	ILECC
Our Facts	. . .	Northampton LEA
Information Handling Pack:	NCET	. . .
Datashow, Our Facts,		
Sorting Game, Branch		
Logo		
Logo	Logotron	Research Machines
Adventure games and simulations		
Lost Frog	ESM	ILECC
Puff	ESM	ILECC
Martello Tower	ESM	ILECC
Merlin's Castle	ESM	ILECC
L	ATM	ATM
Cars – Maths in Motion	Cambridgeshire Software	Cambridgeshire Software
Let's Explore London	Cambridgeshire Software	Cambridgeshire Software
Titanic	ESM	ESM
Factory	ESM	. . .
Games, puzzles and investigations		
MicroSMILE 1: The First 31	ILECC	ILECC
MicroSMILE 2: The Next 17	ILECC	ILECC
MicroSMILE 3: 11 More	ILECC	ILECC
Mathematical Investigations	Capital Media	ILECC
Number Games	Capital Media	ILECC
Number Games	ESM	. . .
Mathematics 9–13	ESM	. . .
Getting Ready for Maths	ESM	. . .
Place Value Activities	ESM	. . .
Maths with a Story 1 and 2	BBC Soft	ILECC
Teaching with a Micro 1 to 5	Shell Centre	Shell Centre
Slimwam 2	ATM	ATM
Shiva Numeracy and Logic	ESM	ESM
Design and drawing packages		
Paintpot	. . .	MUSE
Picture Craft	BBC Soft	ILECC
Mosaic	Advisory Unit	Advisory Unit
Kaleidoscope	ESM	. . .
Frieze	ESM	. . .
Tiling	MUSE	. . .

TEACHING NOTES

Purpose

- To revise multiplication of money
- To introduce decision making in mini-enterprise projects

Materials

Comics, magazines, calculators, stationery catalogue, squared paper.

Vocabulary

Total cost, photocopy, nearest penny, profit, sales, selling price, cost of materials, bar chart, average amount, cheaply, price list, table, advertise, monthly takings, produce, decision

TEACHING POINTS

1 Pounds and pence

Remind the children about the coin and note values used in everyday life and revise the notation for pounds and pence. Ask them to explain why it is important to put the decimal point in the correct place.

Write a number, for example, 425. Ask the children to discover different amounts of money which can be made if the £ sign and decimal point are also used – for example, £425, £4·25.

Give the children practice in writing pence as pounds, and vice versa – for example, 327p → £3·27, £6·20 → 620p.

2 Price lists

Make up a price list of everyday items or use catalogue prices. For example:

Item	Cost
ball	£2·50
music cassette	£6·00
crayons	£1·65
pencil case	£2·25
skates	£12·00

Check that the children can interpret the price list by asking them the cost of the crayons or the pencil case. Then ask which item is the cheapest and which is the dearest, and how many cassettes they could buy for the price of the skates.

A game to play

FIND THE COST

This game can be played in pairs or in two teams.

Use a price list like the one above, and make some cards showing the items to be bought. For example:

> Find the cost of
> 2 balls and
> 1 cassette

Shuffle the cards and turn over the top one. One child has to work out the cost of the items on the card. The second child checks the amount stated using a calculator. One point is scored for each correct amount. No point is scored by the child with the calculator. The children then change over.

The winner is the first player to score 7 points.

3 Rounding

Ask the children to round amounts of money, for example, £1·98 and £5·25 to the nearest pound.

£1·98 → £2·00   £5·25 → £5·00

Explain that amounts such as £5·50 round upwards.

£5·50 → £6·00

Ask them to round amounts to the nearest 10p. For example:

£2·73 → £2·70   £3·55 → £3·60

4 Multiplication of money

Talk about finding the total cost of several things costing the same amount, such as stamps, tickets to the theatre, packets of crisps. For example, the total cost of 7 packets of crisps at 16p each could be written like this:

16p + 16p + 16p + 16p + 16p + 16p + 16p

Ask the children if they can think of a shorter way of writing it. For example:

7 × 16p

There are several ways of recording this. For example:

$$
\begin{array}{c}
£ \\
0.16 \\
\times \quad 7 \\
\hline
1.12
\end{array}
\qquad \text{or} \qquad
\begin{array}{c}
p \\
16 \\
\times \quad 7 \\
\hline
112 = £1.12
\end{array}
$$

A game to play

WORK OUT THE BILL

Put the children in groups of two to five.

Make a price list showing realistic prices of drinks.

Let each group pick out one card and work out the total cost for the group.

This game could be extended by asking a group of four or five children to choose individually one of the three drinks. The total cost for the group is then found.

5 Profit

Talk with the children about making a profit. Explain that if cans or cartons of drinks are sold at a summer fête or in a café, the drinks are often bought from a wholesaler or supermarket (at cost price), amd an amount is added to cover costs and, give a profit. For example, a can costing 20p might be sold at the fête for 25p, giving a possible profit of 5p a can. Ask the children to work out the total profit on selling 5, 10 or 20 cans.

6 Advertising

Ask the children where we see advertisements — for example, on TV, in newspapers, on buses, on hoardings, in shop windows.

Ask which are their favourite advertisements and why.

Explain that manufacturers advertise to inform people about their products so that they might buy them. Similarly, shops advertise to encourage people to spend their money there. In this way the manufacturers and shopkeepers hope to increase their sales and profit.

Point out that the cost of a newspaper advertisement is based on the space taken up by the advert or by the number of words (if it is a small personal advert). Draw a page of a newspaper and show fractional parts such as $\frac{1}{2}, \frac{1}{4}, \frac{1}{8}$.

Ask the children to work out the cost of different sizes of advertisements if a whole page costs £40.

7 Mini-enterprises

Talk with the children about mini-enterprises. Examples might include producing a school magazine, running the school tuck shop, making soft toys and selling them at the school's summer fête, or devising a game and charging people 10p to play it.

Ask groups of children to devise a game to play at a summer fête and suggest a suitable charge. One possible game is to hit a golf ball 5 metres to land on a £5 note to win it. The charge might be 20p a go. Remind them that their game or activity should make a profit, after allowing for overheads.

Ask how many people would have to play before a profit is made.

Explain that often in everyday life the more items you buy, the cheaper they become (because overheads are reduced). Look in catalogues to check this. Ask the children to consider this in planning a mini-enterprise such as sale of apples at break.

8 Mental work

Ask the children mental problems involving multiplication of money, profit, rounding and advertising costs. For example:

A bar of chocolate costs 24p. How much would three bars cost?
A box of chocolates costs £2·40 and is sold for £2·75. How much profit is made?
Round £2·23 to the nearest pound.
A full page advertisement in a newspaper costs £60. How much would a quarter page advert cost?

USING THE CALCULATOR Give the children practice in showing pence as pounds, for example,

$$253p \rightarrow £2·53 \qquad 87p \rightarrow £0·87$$

Give them practice in working out bills in different ways. For example, find the cost for four people at £3·75 each. Ask the children to use both the constant function

$$3·75 + 3·75 + 3·75 + 3·75 = 15·00 \quad (£15·00)$$

and multiplication

$$4 \times 3·75 = 15·00 \quad (£15·00)$$

A game to play

CHECK

Make two sets of cards, one set showing numbers, the other showing prices. One team turns over the top card in each pile.

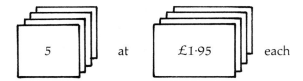

Two players from the other team use a calculator each to work out the answer, one player using the constant function and the other player using multiplication. If the answers 'check' (i.e. are the same) the first time, 1 point is scored. The teams then change over. The first team to score 10 points is the winner.

LINKS WITH THE ENVIRONMENT

Talk about everyday situations where the children might use multiplication of money. These might include:

- bus or train fares
- buying sweets or crisps
- buying stamps
- buying tins of beans or soup
- buying tickets for the theatre, cinema, swimming baths, a football match or school concert
- buying sets of calculators for the class
- mini-enterprises – market stalls, cottage industries, etc.

NOTES ON INVESTIGATIONS

Section A

Check that the children count the number of *sheets* of paper in the comics and magazines rather than the number of pages and, when finding the cost of each sheet, they round the cost to the nearest penny.

The cost of sheets of paper for some comics works out to be about the same, for example, *Dandy* and *Beano*.

Can the children suggest sensible reasons why some comics and magazines cost more per sheet of paper? For example, they may have larger pictures or photographs, stories rather than cartoons, advertisements (which bring money in), or a different quality of paper (e.g. glossy).

Section B

Does the children's magazine include articles, reports, pictures, cartoons, advertisements, etc.?

When working out a price for selling the magazine do they consider the cost of paper, photocopying, glue, etc., and possible income from advertisements? Check that the suggested selling price covers the costs of the materials.

Section C

Check that the children suggest a selling price of more than 40p so that the costs of producing the magazine are covered and that their reasons for the decision are sensible and logical.

Do they allow for a reasonable profit but not overprice with respect to their market? For example, is it better to sell a few magazines at a large profit or many at a small profit? (This idea could be extended by asking the children to do some market research to find how much people would pay for their magazine.)

Do they suggest ways of producing the magazine more cheaply, such as using different quality and sizes of paper, etc.? (Prices could be checked in catalogues.) Additional income from selling advertising space may also be considered.

Shape 1

Purpose

- To introduce rotational symmetry

Materials

Tracing paper, Highway Code, squared paper, templates for hexagons and squares, card, computer (if available)

Vocabulary

Order of rotation, designs, rotational symmetry, triangle, square, rectangle, pentagon, hexagon, octagon, turning design, turning pattern, square pattern

TEACHING POINTS

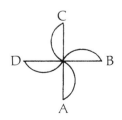

centre of rotation

1 Introducing rotational symmetry

Use a shape which has rotational symmetry or make a windmill.

Talk with the children about the shape, explaining that it can turn about a point called the centre of rotation. Ask them where the centre of rotation is.

Ask how many times the shape could turn and still look exactly the same (four).

This can be shown by marking one 'flag' or using letters A, B, C, D.

Explain that the order of rotational symmetry of the shape is 4.

2 Squared paper shapes

Ask the children to copy shapes like the following onto squared paper and cut them out.

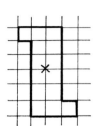 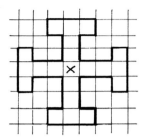

If they put a pin at the centre of rotation and turn the shape, they can find its order of rotation. (It might be necessary to mark one arm of the shape.)

3 Tracing paper designs

Give the children designs which have rotational symmetry. Ask them to trace the designs and turn the tracings.

  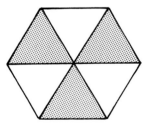

Encourage the children to find the centre of rotation and the order of rotation of each design. If they mark one section of the traced design with a dot or cross, the order of rotation can be found:

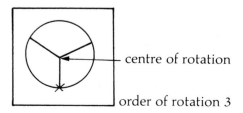

centre of rotation

order of rotation 3

A game to play

CIRCLE DESIGNS

Divide the children into two teams.

Use a circle marked into 12 equal sections (as the 5 minute intervals on a clock face).

Make four sets of cards numbered 2, 3, 4, 6, 12. Shuffle them and place them <u>face</u> down. Ask a child from the first team to turn over a card, e.g. 6. The child has to draw a shape on the circle which has an order of rotation of 6, e.g.

Each correct drawing scores 1 point for the team. The first team to score 6 points wins.

4 Numbers

Write the numbers 1, 2, 3, 4, 5, 6, 7, 8, 9, 0 on the board. Ask the children, which of the numbers have rotational symmetry (1, 8, 0). Discuss 0. Explain that it can have an infinite order of rotation if drawn as a circle; otherwise it usually has order 2. Write the numbers ONE, TWO, etc. on squared paper using capital letters. Ask whether any of the capital letters have rotational symmetry.

5 Order of rotation

Explain that some capital letters, such as J, or shapes, like the one on the left, cannot be turned to look exactly the same except by turning them through 360°. Usually these shapes are said not to have rotational symmetry but it could be argued that they have rotational symmetry of order 1.

6 Computer patterns and designs

Encourage the children to use a computer language such as Logo, Dart or Arrow to produce shapes which have rotational symmetry – for example, an equilateral triangle, a square, a regular pentagon, a regular hexagon, etc. Can the children work out the angle for the amount of turn correctly? For example:

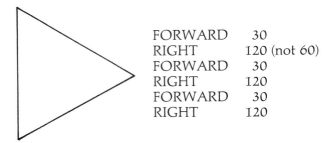

FORWARD	30
RIGHT	120 (not 60)
FORWARD	30
RIGHT	120
FORWARD	30
RIGHT	120

Talk about the link between the commands that can be repeated and the order of rotation of the shape. For example, the above shape could be produced by

REPEAT 3 TIMES
FORWARD 30
RIGHT 120
END

The equilateral triangle has an order of rotation of 3.
    NB. The commands for Logo, Dart and Arrow vary slightly.

7 More complex designs

Explain that a shape can be made into a pattern or design which has rotational symmetry by turning it a number of times to make exactly 360°. Ask the children to use a template or a computer language such as Logo, Dart or Arrow to make patterns.
    Possible examples include the following. (NB. When using the computer, TRIANGLE must be built first.)

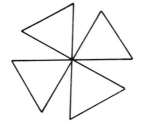

Using the computer
REPEAT 4
TRIANGLE
RIGHT 90
END

Using a template
Repeat this 4 times. Draw an equilateral triangle. Turn it through 90°.

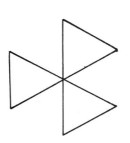

Using the computer
REPEAT 3
TRIANGLE
RIGHT 120
END

Using a template
Repeat this 3 times. Draw an equilateral triangle. Turn it through 120°.

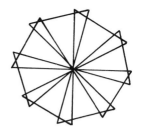

Using the computer
REPEAT 8
TRIANGLE
RIGHT 45
END

Using a template
Repeat this 8 times. Draw an equilateral triangle. Turn it through 45°.

Similar examples to these are in section C of the pupils' book. Squared paper, isometric paper or a sheet of paper with the angles accurately marked would be useful if the computer is not being used.

LINKS WITH THE ENVIRONMENT

Talk about everyday situations, patterns and designs involving rotational symmetry. Possibilities include:

- road signs (see the Highway Code)
- car symbols — Opel, Mercedes, BMW, British Leyland
- cars — wheel covers, steering wheels
- lettering in shop signs
- umbrellas
- symbols for major companies or organisations — wool sign, Aer Lingus, Isle of Man, British Rail
- stained glass windows, grids
- the big wheel at a fairground
- nature — (although may not be perfect) flower heads, starfish

NOTES ON INVESTIGATIONS

Section A

Check that the children select road signs from the Highway Code which have rotational symmetry of order more than 1. Possible examples include the no entry sign, no vehicle sign, the level crossing sign, a meter zone sign. They should write the order of rotation of each.

Do their invented signs all have rotational symmetry?

Section B

The children's capital letters patterns should have rotational symmetry of order 2 or order 4. One way to make a turning pattern with rotational symmetry of order 2 is to draw any capital letter, turn it through 180° and draw it again. Similarly, drawing any capital letter, turning it through 90°, 180°, 270° and drawing it each time will produce patterns with rotational symmetry order 4.

Section C

If a computer is available, the children could use it to draw their patterns.

Check that the hexagonal patterns all have rotational symmetry. Can the children describe their patterns and state the order of rotation? They might spot the relationship between the order of rotation and the angle the shape has turned through:

order 2 $360° \div 2 = 180°$
order 3 $360° \div 3 = 120°$
order 4 $360° \div 4 = 90°$
order 5 $360° \div 5 = 72°$ etc.

Do they make turning patterns with rotational symmetry using other shapes?

Number 1

Purpose

- To introduce multiplication of ThHTU by one digit
- To introduce division of ThHTU by one digit
- To give practice in using inverse operations to check answers
- To introduce reading a calculator display to the nearest whole number
- To give experience in recognising rounding errors on the calculator

Materials

Calculators; an educational supplier's catalogue may be useful for reference

Vocabulary

Cubes, equally, half, calculator, whole number, nearest whole number, predict, dividing, multiplying, gross, estimate, divide exactly, quire, ream, approximately, methods

TEACHING POINTS   **1 Multiplication and division patterns**

Remind the children how to make multiplication and division patterns by grouping the numbers into 7s, 8s, 9s, etc. Ask them to complete the pattern of 8s and to draw the pattern of 9s.

1	2	3	4	5	6	7	8
9	10	11	12	13	14	15	16
17	18						

Ask questions such as

$$5 \times 8 = \square \quad \text{or} \quad 40 \div 8 = \square$$

Ask the children to count in 8s around the class. They must try to 'keep the kettle boiling'. If anyone is too slow in answering or gives an incorrect answer, they are 'out'.

Do the same for other multiplication patterns.

2 Multiplication square

Remind the children how to use the multiplication square as a ready reckoner.

3 Revision of tables

Give the children plenty of practice in revising their tables. Play games such as matching tables flash cards to their answers as quickly as possible.

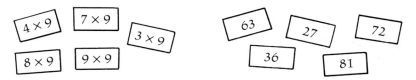

Remind children how to use their fingers to show their 9 × tables. For example:

$$2 \times 9 = 18$$

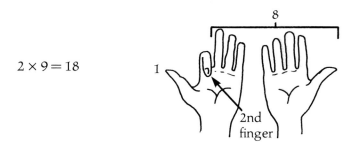

4 Rules of divisibility

It might be useful, too, to remind the children of the rules of divisibility which they have met. If the digits of a number add up to a multiple of 3, then that number is exactly divisible by 3. The 2s pattern ends in 2, 4, 6, 8, 0 and the 5s pattern ends in 5 or 0.

An interesting investigation on divisibility involves a number and its reverse. In these two examples if we subtract the answer is divisible by 9, while if we add the answer is divisible by 11.

$$\begin{array}{r} 61 \\ -16 \\ \hline 45 \end{array} \ (\div 9) \qquad \begin{array}{r} 61 \\ +16 \\ \hline 77 \end{array} \ (\div 11)$$

Ask the children to investigate if this applies to other two-digit numbers, or to three-digit numbers.

5 Linking multiplication and division (inverse operations)

Give the children revision practice in this. For example:

$$8 \times 7 = 56$$
$$7 \times 8 = 56$$
$$56 \div 7 = 8$$
$$56 \div 8 = 7$$

Point out that this can be very useful in checking multiplication or division calculations.

The idea of a function machine may help to reinforce this:

Let the children practice with larger numbers using a calculator.

Remind the children that there is also the link between addition and subtraction, and encourage them to use inverse operations when checking their work. For example,

42	69	42	42
+ 27	− 27	6)252	× 6
69	42		252

6 Multiplication of ThHTU by one digit

Use your own words and methods to show the children how to multiply ThHTU by one digit and how to record their work. Structural apparatus may be useful to remind the children about 'carrying'.

Encourage the children to suggest alternative methods. For example,

$1200 \times 6 \rightarrow$

```
    1200      or   6 × 1000 = 6000
    1200           6 ×  200 = 1200
    1200
    1200           6 × 1200 = 7200
    1200
  + 1200

    7200
```

What do the children think are the advantages or disadvantages of the different methods? Which do they prefer to use? Give them plenty of practice, using their preferred method.

7 Division of ThHTU by one digit

Begin by reminding the children how to divide HTU by one digit. Then use structural apparatus to show them how to divide ThHTU by one digit. For example:

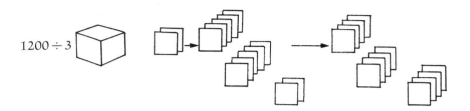

$$1200 \div 3$$

Give the children plenty of practice in this.
Talk to them about 'exchanging', different methods of recording, and how to work out division problems such as $1200 \div 3$.
Again, give the children plenty of practice.

Games to play

DIVIDE IT

Write a division problem on the board, e.g. $1400 \div 2$.
Ask two small groups of children to each show the division using structural apparatus. The first group to show this correctly is the winner.

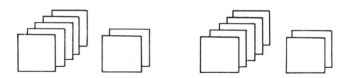

An alternative game is to use structural apparatus to give the answer to the problem. The first group to write the division to fit the answer (i.e. $1400 \div 2$) is the winner.

REMAINDER RACE

Three children play the game; a fourth child has a list of answers to check that the game is played correctly.
The game requires counters and flash cards of divisions with remainders of 1, 2 or 3. (There will need to be an equal number of cards for each remainder.) The level of difficulty of the flash cards should be matched to the capability and experience of the children.
The three players decide who will be 'Remainder 1, 2 or 3'. The flash cards are shuffled and placed downwards in a pile. The cards

are turned over one at a time and the children must decide if the answer has a remainder of 1, 2 or 3. If the answer has a remainder of 2 (for example 10 ÷ 4) the 'Remainder 2' player collects a counter. The game continues until the winner collects 4 counters.

When all the cards have been used they can be reshuffled and placed face down on the table to be played again.

8 Rounding

Remind the children how to round numbers to get approximate numbers, and how 5, 50 or 500 always round up to the nearest 10, 100 or 1000.

Draw a chart on the board.

Number	Nearest 10	Nearest 100	Nearest 1000
2462			

Choose three teams and allocate a column of the chart to each one, for example, team 1 might have the 'nearest 10' column. Write a number on the chart, e.g. 2462. A member from each team has to round 2462 up or down according to the requirements of their column, and write the answers on the chart. Each correct answer scores a point for the team.

Talk to the children about when it is useful to round numbers, such as when estimating answers in order to check approximate accuracy. For example:

$$1473 - 382 \text{ is about } 1100$$

Let them investigate pairs of numbers to see which approximate totals are closest to the true ones. For example:

$$2460 + 1894 \rightarrow 2000 + 2000 \rightarrow 4000 \quad \text{True total} = 4354$$
$$2460 + 1574 \rightarrow 2000 + 2000 \rightarrow 4000 \quad \text{True total} = 4034$$

Can they begin to predict which estimated totals will be close to the true ones?

Give the children practice in estimating totals by approximating. For example, ask them to estimate, by rounding to the nearest 1000, which pair of numbers gives a total nearest to 3000.

9 Nearest whole number

Talk about what is meant by whole numbers, and ask for examples of numbers that aren't, for example, $3\frac{1}{2}$, 4·5, etc.

Remind the children that when solving division problems using a calculator, the remainder is shown as a number or numbers after the point. The number to the left of the point is the whole number.

Give the children practice in using the calculator to divide by 2 and 5. Write some of the calculations on the board.

$$16 \div 5 = 3 \cdot 2$$

Talk about rounding this answer to the nearest whole number. Explain that 0·2 is really $\frac{2}{10}$. Draw a number line to show its position.

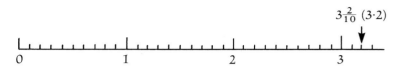

$3\frac{2}{10}$ (3·2)

0   1   2   3

Point out that by convention 0·5 is always rounded up to the next whole number.

Give the children practice in positioning numbers on the line, for example, 2·4, 3·6. Ask them to round each one to the nearest whole number.

Give the children practice in dividing by 4 and 8 on their calculators. Explain that 2·25 is $2\frac{25}{100}$. Can they round this to the nearest whole number? Give the children plenty of practice in this.

The investigation in section A involves division by 3 so it would be useful to let the children experience what happens when they divide by 3, 6 or 9 on the calculator and the answer is not a whole number. Can they suggest how to round the answer to the nearest whole number?

A game to play

NEAREST WHOLE NUMBER

Call out a number for the children to display on their calculators, for example 452·6. The first to give you the nearest whole number scores a point.

Play the game again, but this time with numbers to two decimal places.

MENTAL WORK

- Revise division bonds such as $56 \div 7$, $64 \div 8$. Ask questions about them such as 'How many 9s in 72?' 'What do we divide by 8 to get an answer of 6?'
- Ask the children verbal division problems.
- Ask questions that involve remainders.
- Give an answer, for example, 2 rem 4. Ask the children to give you possible divisions that fit it.
- Give the children practice in rounding numbers to the nearest 10, 100, 1000.

USING THE CALCULATOR

Remind the children how the calculator shows that a number does not divide exactly. Give them plenty of opportunity to observe this on their own calculators.

Give the children plenty of practice in displaying numbers with one or two decimal places on their calculators. Let them round them to the nearest whole numbers.

A game to play

PREDICT THE REMAINDER

Divide some children into two groups. Give a child in the first group a division which involves a remainder, for example, $29 \div 4$, $331 \div 2$, $224 \div 5$. (The level of difficulty obviously depends on the ability of the children.) Ask them to predict whether there is a remainder — yes or no. A member from the second group checks on a calculator whether the prediction is right or wrong. If the prediction is correct, the player who made it scores a point.

The game continues until all the players in both groups have had a turn at predicting.

LINKS WITH THE ENVIRONMENT

Talk with the children about situations which involve sharing and grouping.

- Team or group games. When the class is put into teams or groups, what happens to the 'extra' children?
- Talk about sharing equipment or materials out in school, clubs, or among teams.
- Discuss when it helps to round to the nearest whole numbers, for example, when estimating averages, predicting school fund-raising totals, interest rates $14\cdot8\% \rightarrow 15\%$.

NOTES ON INVESTIGATIONS

Section A

The children should find that $? \div 4 \times 4$ cancels itself out (i.e. $\div 4$ is the inverse of $\times 4$) so $8 \div 4 \times 4$ gives the answer 8. By the same reasoning, do they predict that $7 \div 3 \times 3$ gives the answer 7?

They may find that, on some calculators, $7 \div 3 \times 3$ gives an answer of $6\cdot999\,999\,9$ (i.e. $6\cdot9$ recurring). This does not happen with $\div 2 \times 2$ and $\div 4 \times 4$ but can happen with $\div 3 \times 3$ on a calculator when the number being divided gives a recurring decimal and multiplying by 3 does not give the original number. The children could investigate other numbers, for example $\div 7 \times 7$, when the same thing happens. For example, $5 \div 7 \times 7$ gives $4\cdot999\,999\,9$ on some calculators. They may discover that it does not happen if the multiplication is done first and then followed by the division. For example:

$$5 \times 7 \div 7 = 5$$

but

$$5 \div 7 \times 7 = 4 \cdot 999\,999$$

Section B

Discuss with the children how they approached the problem. Did they use a logical approach? For example, they could find all the multiples of 6 and 8 up to 200 on a calculator and then look for the numbers common to both lists. Another possibility is to mark off the pattern of 6 and 8 on a hundred square and look for numbers that coincide.

Perhaps the quickest way is to find the smallest number that both 6 and 8 divide into exactly and then count on in multiples of that number:

24   48   72   96   120   144   168   192

Do the children realise that the pattern increases by 24 each time, and that all the numbers are even?

Section C

The children should soon appreciate that they cannot accurately measure the thickness of one sheet of paper. Practical methods could include:

(a) measuring, in cm, the thickness of 100 sheets and then dividing by 100 using a calculator.
(b) stacking a 10 mm (1 cm) pile of sheets of paper, counting the sheets, then dividing 10 mm by the number of sheets, using a calculator.

Length

Purpose

- To understand the use of scale in drawings
- To draw plans using simple scales

Materials

Squared paper, ruler, simple plans of the school, houses, safari parks, etc.

Vocabulary

Plan, scale, length, width, perimeter, scale drawing, measurements, nearest, accurately, scale plans

TEACHING POINTS

1 Using plans

Discuss with the children the use of scale plans, how they show a picture, usually smaller, of the object or site. For example, a scale plan of a safari park could indicate where the animals are. Plans of homes are sometimes shown in estate agents' windows so that house features and sizes can be judged without having to visit the site. A school plan is often put up at the school entrance so parents can see where classrooms are.

2 Explaining scale

Explain that scale drawings and plans are usually drawn many times smaller than life size for convenience of handling and using. Each plan has its own scale.

3 A plan of the classroom

Talk with the children about how they would draw a plan of the classroom. Discuss how first it is necessary to find the true measurements and then to suggest a scale that conveniently fits on a sheet of paper.

4 Using the 1 cm : 1 m scale

Discuss how a useful scale is where 1 cm represents 1 metre. This can be written as 1 cm : 1 m.

Let a pair of children measure the length and width of the classroom to the nearest metre. Write the measurements on the board and ask the children how many centimetres long they would draw the length and width of the room if they were using a 1 cm: 1 m scale.

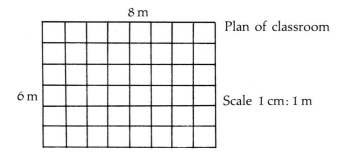

8 m

Plan of classroom

6 m

Scale 1 cm: 1 m

5 Using squared paper

Give the children a sheet of squared (cm) paper and ask them to draw a plan of the classroom, showing the scale.

6 A plan of the hall

Let a pair of children measure the length and width of the hall to the nearest metre. Ask the children to draw a scale plan on squared paper, using a scale of 1 cm: 1 m.

7 Using a 1 cm: 2 m scale

Talk to the children about using a 1 cm: 2 m scale for larger measurements such as a netball or soccer pitch. Ask what the length of a 100 m × 50 m pitch would be on a plan drawn to a scale of 1 cm: 2 m. Let the children draw it on squared paper.

8 Other sports pitches

Let the children suggest other sports pitches, find their dimensions and draw them to a scale of 1 cm: 2 m or 1 cm: 1 m, whichever is more appropriate.

MENTAL WORK   Ask the children to work out the distance on a map, given the scale and actual distance on the ground. For example, on a scale of 1 cm: 2 m, how far on the map is 40 m on the ground?

**LINKS WITH THE
ENVIRONMENT**

- Look at tourist maps and town guides.
- Ask the children to measure rooms in their homes and draw a scale plan, using a suitable scale.

**NOTES ON
INVESTIGATIONS**

Section A

The children should draw plans of a variety of pools, each with a perimeter of 40 cm. They may develop a system using pattern for deciding upon dimensions. For example:

Length	Width	Perimeter
10	10	40
11	9	40
12	8	40

Do they draw some pools that are not rectangles?

Section B

The children should first carefully measure the hall and then approximate to the nearest metre. They need to decide upon a sensible surround for the pool, for example, a minimum of a 2 m width all the way round the pool. Then they should draw the scale plan on squared paper, choosing an appropriate scale to fill most of the paper.

Section C

The children should measure the diagram of the pool and find that it is approximately in proportion 2:1. Do they choose realistic dimensions for a garden pool (say 6 m in length) and a park lake (say 60 m in length)? Do they choose a suitable scale for each drawing?

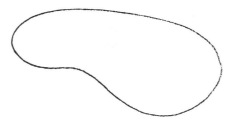

Purpose

- To find the area of composite shapes using cm²

Materials

Squared paper, geoboards, dotted paper (cm²)

Vocabulary

Area, cm², length, width, height, perimeter, measurements, approximately, exact area, accurately, rectangle

TEACHING POINTS

1 Recording area

Remind the children that area is the amount of surface covered by a shape and that standard units for measuring are the square centimetre, written as cm², and the square metre, written as m².

2 Area of rectangular shapes

Draw a rectangular shape and show the measurements and squares. Remind the children about the length and width of rectangles. Point out that we sometimes refer to the height and width instead of length and width, for example of windows.

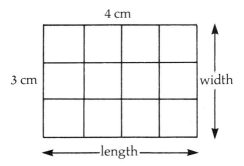

Ask the children how many centimetre squares cover the rectangle, and therefore what its area is.

Ask them to draw other rectangles on squared paper. Write on the measurements, and find their areas. (It is probably better, for the sake of accuracy, if the children use squared paper.)

Can the children suggest a 'quick way' of finding the area? For example:

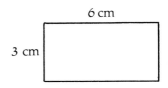

$$L \times W = A,$$

(They were asked to find the relationship between length, width and area in Module 6 Book 2.) Encourage them to use this 'quick way' when tackling the work in the pupils' books, although a few children may still find it more helpful to count centimetre squares.

Give the children experience in finding the area in m² too, although this is not encountered in the pupils' pages. Perhaps they could find the area of rectangular rooms in school. Ask them to find the measurements of the rooms to the nearest metre first.

3 Further work on area

Ask the children to draw rectangles of given areas, for example, 15 cm², 24 cm². As an alternative, give the area and one other measurement, for example,

area = 20 cm²,   width = 5 cm

Ask them to draw the shape and write on the length measurement.

4 Geoboards and dotted paper

Encourage the children to use geoboards and dotted paper as aids to finding the area of rectangular shapes.

A game to play

WHAT'S MISSING?

This game can be played in two or more groups. Give each group two cards (they need not necessarily be the same for each group). One card shows the area of a rectangle. The other card shows either the width or length.

The groups can use squared paper, geoboards or dotted paper to work out the missing width measurement. The first group to give you the correct missing measurement for their 'area' scores a point.

Area
30 cm²

Length
10 cm

5 Area of composite shapes

Talk about the shapes of rooms in school or at home. Can they think of any rooms that are not rectangular? Draw a plan of one of them on the board, for example:

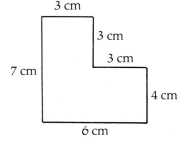

Can the children suggest any ways of finding the area, by dividing it into two rectangles? How would they find the area of the whole shape?

Give the children practice in making irregular shapes using two rectangles. Make some cardboard rectangles of varying sizes and ask them to find different ways of arranging them in pairs to make composite shapes. They could blu-tak their final shape on the board for everyone to see. For example:

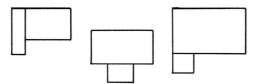

The rectangles could also be made from activity paper or newspaper. Geoboards and spotted paper can again be used to give practice in dividing irregular shapes into rectangles.

6 Calculating the area of composite shapes

Use squared paper. Ask the children to draw an 'L' shape of given measurements (for example, the shape given at the start of activity 5). Ask them to divide it into two rectangles, find the area of each one and then find the area of the whole shape. Can they record what they have done? (They may need to colour or label the shapes to identify them.)

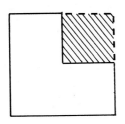

Can they suggest another way of calculating the area of the 'L' shape, by subtraction?

Area of the whole shape is ___ cm²
Area of the shaded shape is ___ cm²
Area of the 'L' shape is ___ cm²

Let them draw a plan of a garden, divided into rectangles according to its usage and work out the total area, for example:

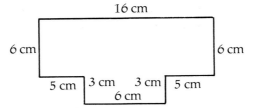

A calculator may be useful when the numbers begin to get bigger.

Give them practice in finding the area of composite shapes in m², for example, the area of the classroom without the stockroom. The measurements will be to the nearest metre.

7 Missing measurements

Point out that shapes do not always have every measurement written on. Draw some shapes on the board and ask the children to find the missing measurements. Ask them to explain how they worked them out.

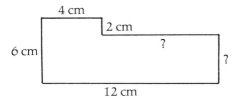

A game to play

FIND THE MEASUREMENTS

This game can be played in two small groups. Draw four different composite shapes, each one on a separate paper or card. Show all but one or two of the measurements on each shape.
Give the two groups an identical set of cards.
Which group can find all the missing measurements first?

8 What's left?

Give the children a rectangular piece of art paper; its measurements must be in whole centimetres. Give them some smaller rectangles of coloured gummed paper; again the measurements must be in whole centimetres. Ask the children to make a design on the art paper using two or three of the smaller rectangles, which must not overlap.
    Talk with them about the area of the whole art paper and the area of the design. Can they suggest a way of finding out the area of the art paper not covered by the design?

9 Revise perimeters

Remind the children that a perimeter is the distance round the edge or boundary of a shape. Ask them to walk round the perimeter of the skittle ball pitch, football pitch, playground or the school. Remind them how to measure the perimeter of smaller things to the nearest centimetre, and give them practice in doing this.
    Talk about finding the perimeter of a shape like a rectangle using 'doubling'. For example:

$(2 \times 9 \text{ cm}) + (2 \times 4 \text{ cm}) = 26 \text{ cm}$

10 Area and perimeter

Ask the children to draw shapes which each have an area of 5 cm²
and a perimeter of 12 cm, for example:

Can they draw one with the same area but a different perimeter? For
example:

MENTAL WORK

- Ask the children questions about perimeters of regular shapes.
  For example, if each side of a hexagon is 4 cm, what is its
  perimeter?
- Give addition practice, for example, quick additions by looking
  for easy number bonds (e.g. $8 + 10 + 8 + 10 = 20 + 16 = 36$).
- Revise addition and subtraction links, for example,

  $$24 - \square = 14 \quad 14 + \square = 24$$

  and addition and multiplication links, for example,

  $$9 + 9 + 9 + 9 = 4 \times 9 = 36$$

- Practise doubling numbers, for example,

  $$14 + 8 + 14 + 8 = (2 \times 8) + (2 \times 14) = 44$$

- Find the difference between two areas.
- Ask questions about the area of shapes. For example, if the area
  of a shape is 20 cm² and its width is 4 cm, what is its length?

LINKS WITH THE ENVIRONMENT

Talk with the children about where they might measure area in
square centimetres.

- The area covered by a picture or design in a magazine or on a
  poster
- The floor, wall, door, or window areas on a plan or model
- The area taken by a stamp on an envelope
- The area taken up by an advertisement, picture or cartoon in a
  newspaper

Talk about areas which would be measured in square metres.

- Area of fields
- Area of floors for carpeting or tiling
- The area of their house and garden

Look in carpet shops for prices per m², and calculate the cost of carpeting the classroom or a bedroom.

NOTES ON INVESTIGATIONS

Section A

The children could use the technique of splitting the shape into rectangles in various ways. For example:

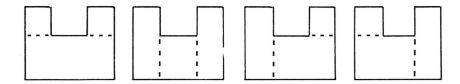

Section B

The smallest area is 7 cm² and the greatest is 16 cm², for shapes with straight sides that are a whole number of centimetres. Half centimetres might also be considered.

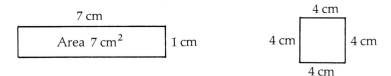

A circle of circumference 16 cm gives the greatest area.

Section C

Do the children realise that the area of the rectangle is 20 cm² so each of the four shapes must have an area of 5 cm²? For example:

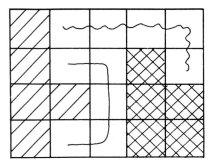
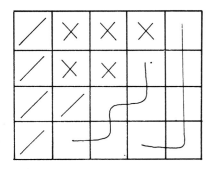

Purpose

- To find volumes by counting cubes
- To give practice in calculating volumes
- To introduce the cubic centimetre (cm³)

Materials

Centimetre cubes, large squared paper, card or strong paper to make boxes, soap powder boxes (E3 and other sizes)

Vocabulary

Volume, cubic centimetres, cuboids, centimetre, cubes, cm³, measurements, length, width, height, possible measurements, predict, larger, diameter, design, squared paper

TEACHING POINTS

1 Volume of boxes

Remind the children that the volume of a box is the amount of space it occupies or takes up. Discuss how to measure this space, i.e. with cubes, and why cubes are the best units for measuring volume, rather than marbles for example.

Children may need practical experience of this using larger cubes before moving on to cubic centimetres.

2 The centimetre cube

Let the children look carefully at some centimetre cubes. What can they tell you about them? Do they realise that each side is 1 cm long, hence the name?

3 Cubic centimetres

Talk with the children about how volume may be measured in cubic centimetres. A centimetre cube has a volume of 1 cubic centimetre or 1 cm³, so centimetre cubes can be used to find the volume of objects such as boxes.

4 Using centimetre cubes

Talk about using centimetre cubes to measure and how the answer can often only be an approximate one. Can the children think why?

Give the children some small boxes or containers, for example matchboxes or stock-cube boxes. First, they should estimate approximately how many centimetre cubes each one will hold. Then they fill the boxes with centimetre cubes to find approximate volumes. How close were the children's estimates?

5 Further practice in measuring volume

Talk to the children about volume being the amount of space occupied or taken up by a shape.

Ask them to make a cuboid using centimetre cubes. Its measurements are length 2 cm, width 2 cm, height 3 cm.

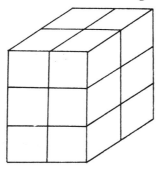

How many centimetre cubes do they use? Can they tell you its volume?

This work is repeated in the activities in section A in the chapter but the extra practice is very useful in understanding the concept.

6 Vocabulary

At this point it may be useful to remind the children what is meant by length, width and height.

A game to play

LABEL THE BOXES

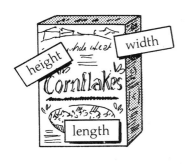

This game is for two groups.

Make several labels for each of 'length', 'height', 'width'.

Give each group a selection of boxes. At a given signal the groups label the length, width, and height of each box using blu-tak or sticky tape. The first group to label all their boxes correctly is the winner. They can then remove the labels and exchange boxes to see who wins the next time.

Question what happens if the boxes are turned. Should the labels be changed?

7 Calculating volume

Talk with the children about the practicalities of using centimetre cubes to measure the volumes of larger boxes. How many cubes would they need?

Build some cuboids, for example:

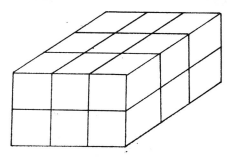

length = 3 cm   width = 3 cm   height = 2 cm   volume = 18 cm³

Can they devise a way of calculating the volume without using centimetre cubes?

Give the children plenty of examples to discuss and to calculate the volumes.

Give them the volume, for example 12 cm³, and ask them to use cubes to make a cuboid of that volume and to write its measurements. If they calculate the volume using these measurements, do they get 12 cm³?

Talk about how boxes can be different shaped cuboids and yet still have the same volume.

A game to play

MAKE A BOX

This can be played in two or more groups, or in two teams.
Give the volume of a box, for example, 16 cm³. The first group or player who can give you a set of length, width and height measurements to make the volume scores a point.

8 Made to measure

Talk about how the volume of boxes or containers depend on what they have to contain.

Look at everyday objects in school, for example a PE ball, and how the children would design a box for it.

Can they suggest ways of finding the measurements for the box? For example, they could put the ball between two piles of books,

leaving a small gap at either side, then measure the distance between the books to find the length and width. Next they would measure the height needed, again remembering to leave a small gap.

Can they calculate the approximate volume of the box?

Investigate the designs and volumes needed to box other classroom objects. A calculator may be very useful here, with the possible larger numbers.

9 Volume in the environment

Talk to the children about the importance of volume when designing animal homes, for example, rabbit hutches, fish tanks, crates and boxes for transporting animals. Discuss how the volume of the container must allow for the animal's comfort and well-being.

The RSPCA gives guidelines about the size of animal homes.

- A cage for a pair of mice – floor space at least 1200 cm^2 (i.e. 30 cm × 40 cm), height 30 cm
- Indoor rabbit hutch – floor space at least 7200 cm^2, minimum height 60 cm
- Hamster cage – floor space at least 2400 cm^2, height 30 cm
- Gerbil cage – floor space at least 1500 cm^2, height 30 cm

The children might enjoy working out the recommended volumes with the aid of a calculator and comparing them with their pets' homes.

MENTAL WORK

- Give the children practice in multiplying three digits, for example,

  $2 \times 3 \times 4$

- Give them practice in looking for the easy ways of multiplying, for example,

  $2 \times 4 \times 5 \rightarrow (2 \times 5) \times 4$

  Remind them that multiplication is associative by asking questions such as

  $2 \times 3 \times 2 = \square$
  $2 \times 2 \times 3 = \square$
  $3 \times 2 \times 2 = \square$

- Ask them to find the missing number, for example,

  $2 \times 3 \times \square = 12$

- Ask problems about finding the volume of cuboids, given the height, length and width.

**USING THE
CALCULATOR** Let the children investigate multiplication of three numbers in any order, for example

$$5 \times 7 \times 4 = \square \qquad 4 \times 5 \times 7 = \square$$

What do they notice? Does the same apply to larger numbers?

Can they use their calculators to devise a way of finding missing numbers? For example

$$6 \times \square \times 5 = 210$$

Give them plenty of practice in this.

Give the children a number, for example 120. Can they find two numbers that multiply together to make it? Can they find three numbers?

Ask them to find the length of the edge of a cube whose volume is 64 cm³ using trial and improvement methods. Do the same for a cube of volume 216 cm³.

A game to play

GROUPINGS

The children work in pairs.
They can use the numbers 1, 2, 3, 4, and the × sign.
Ask them to arrange the numbers into groups of three and multiply them to make 144, 246, 92, for example

$$12 \times 3 \times 4 \rightarrow 36 \times 4 \rightarrow 144$$

Which pair can give the correct answer first?

**LINKS WITH THE
ENVIRONMENT**
- Look at boxes and containers in shops.
- Look at boxes containing books or equipment when they are delivered at school.
- Look at the boxes which hold or transport unusually shaped objects, for example, perfume bottles or museum objects on loan to school, such as a Roman helmet. Talk about how they are designed so that there is very little wasted space.
- Packaging – talk about how the volume of boxes has to leave room for packaging when carrying fragile objects.
- Let the children design and make a cage for an animal of their choice in design and technology.

Section A

Do the children look for a pattern or system for finding lengths, widths and heights to give a volume of 36 cm³? They could draw up a chart, or consider the factors of 36.

Length	Width	Height	Volume
36 cm	1 cm	1 cm	36 cm³
18 cm	1 cm	2 cm	36 cm³
18 cm	2 cm	1 cm	36 cm³
9 cm	4 cm	1 cm	36 cm³
9 cm	1 cm	4 cm	etc.

Section B

Do the children see the patterns of

$$1 \text{ cm} \times 1 \text{ cm} \times 1 \text{ cm} = 1 \text{ cm}^3$$
$$2 \text{ cm} \times 2 \text{ cm} \times 2 \text{ cm} = 8 \text{ cm}^3$$
$$3 \text{ cm} \times 3 \text{ cm} \times 3 \text{ cm} = 27 \text{ cm}^3$$
$$4 \text{ cm} \times 4 \text{ cm} \times 4 \text{ cm} = 64 \text{ cm}^3$$
$$5 \text{ cm} \times 5 \text{ cm} \times 5 \text{ cm} = 125 \text{ cm}^3$$

Do they predict that the next two larger cubes will be as follows?

$$6 \text{ cm} \times 6 \text{ cm} \times 6 \text{ cm} = 216 \text{ cm}^3$$
$$7 \text{ cm} \times 7 \text{ cm} \times 7 \text{ cm} = 343 \text{ cm}^3$$

Section C

Do the children calculate the volumes of the E15 and E3 boxes and find, possibly by trial and improvement, that the volume of the E15 is approximately five times greater than the E3? Do they relate this to the weight of powder in each box and discover that the E15 holds five times more (6 kg to 1·2 kg)? Do they investigate the E10 box and discover a similar relationship for weight and volume?

Probability 1

Purpose

- To understand and use a probability scale from 0 to 1
- To estimate the probabilities of a range of events and justify them.

Materials

Squared paper, ruler

Vocabulary

Chance, likelihood, probability scale, certain, no chance, impossible, Victorian

TEACHING POINTS

1 Revising certain and impossible

Revise the fact that some events are certain and some are impossible. Ask the children to make a list of such events. For example:

Certain	Impossible
It will go dark tonight I will breathe today	I will be twice as tall tomorrow

2 Introducing the 0 to 1 possibility scale

Explain that every event can be put on a probability scale from 0 to 1, where 0 is impossible (or has 'no chance' of happening) and 1 is certain. Ask the children to make up some events which would fit on the scale at 0 or 1.

```
0                                                    1
|_____|
No chance                                        Certain
```

3 The half-way point

Discuss what sort of events would be placed at the half-way mark on the 0 to 1 probability scale. Discuss the likelihood of an event taking place if it is (correctly) placed mid-way between 0 and 1; it

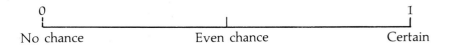

4 Even chance

Discuss what is meant by an even chance. For example, the chance of spinning a coin and getting a head is neither 'no chance' nor 'certain' — it is exactly half-way between the two probabilities. Throwing a head has an even chance.

5 Other even chances

Ask the children to list other events that have an even chance. These might include:

- the chance of throwing an odd number with an ordinary dice.
- the chance of drawing a red card from a shuffled pack of six red cards and six blue cards.

6 Other probabilities

Discuss the probability of a particular child being in school tomorrow. The probability is high, but not certain because they might become ill, etc. It is almost certain, so it is placed near the 'certain' end in the 'good chance' range of the 0 to 1 probability scale.

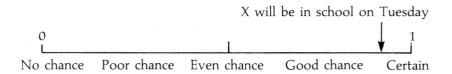

Point out that the event cannot be placed in an exact spot but we must make the best estimate we can.

Ask the children where they would place the event if they didn't feel very well today, and then if they felt very unwell today. Discuss the 'poor chance' range.

Probability that I will be at school tomorrow

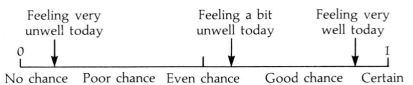

7 Place the event

Draw a probability scale on the board. Ask the children to write six events that will fit at points along the scale and discuss them with others, justifying their positioning of the events. For example:

> 'It will rain today' is very likely because it is only morning and the sky is already looking darker.
> I will put this event along the good chance range

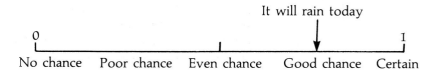

8 Writing probabilities

Discuss with the children that if 0 is 'no chance' and 1 is 'certain' then 'even chance' is $\frac{1}{2}$, or 1 chance out of 2. So the chance of throwing a head with a coin can be said to be 1 out of 2 or $\frac{1}{2}$.

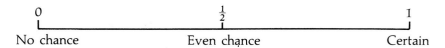

9 Other probabilities

Discuss what other fractions may show probabilities. For example, the probability of throwing a 5 on a dice is 1 out of 6 or $\frac{1}{6}$. Ask children where this would go on the 0 to 1 probability scale. $\frac{1}{6}$ is less than an even chance it will be in the 'poor chance' range. It must be $\frac{1}{6}$ of the scale along from 0.

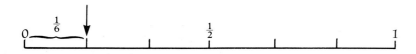

Point out that the scale can be divided into any number of parts; it is often divided into 10 parts.

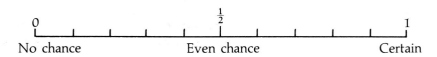

LINKS WITH THE
ENVIRONMENT

- Ask the children to estimate, and justify, probabilities of events throughout the day. For example, 'we will have play-time at 10:30 a.m. today', 'the paper will be delivered in the morning', 'the moon will be seen tonight'.
- Ask the children to compile a list of things that they are certain will happen today and a list of things that will not happen today.

NOTES ON
INVESTIGATIONS

Section A

Encourage the children to devise both likely and unlikely events, so that they use the full range of the probability scale. For example:

A   We will get changed.
B   We will sing in PE.
C   We will use PE hoops.

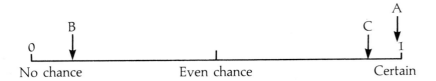

Section B

Do the children appreciate that a likelihood of $\frac{9}{10}$ is close to being certain? Check that they give sensible reasons to justify this high probability. For example: at holiday times there are a lot of cars on the road so traffic jams are almost certain.

Do they make up logical possibilities from bus, train and car travel and assign appropriate probability fractions to them? For example: the train to the seaside is likely to be very full during holiday times if it is good weather.

Section C

The children should devise a range of activities with different probabilities and show them on appropriate scales. (Squared paper may be useful.) For example:

1   I will throw a 4 on a die ($\frac{1}{6}$)
2   My friend was born on a Tuesday ($\frac{1}{7}$)
3   I will draw a 4 from a pack of 0–9 flash cards ($\frac{1}{10}$)
4   I will guess the correct answer in a multiple-choice set of questions (1/number of questions)
5   My chance of drawing an ace from a full pack of cards is $\frac{4}{52} = \frac{1}{13}$.

Map reading

Purpose

- To specify location by means of co-ordinates
- To locate features on an Ordnance Survey map, using grid references

Materials

Squared paper, variety of maps (including Ordnance Survey maps)

Vocabulary

Easting, northing, grid reference, grid, symbol, scale, shortest distance, direction, features

TEACHING POINTS

1 What is a map?

Introduce or revise the idea that a map is the picture that you might see from overhead if you were a bird or in an aeroplane. Ask how a house might look to a bird.

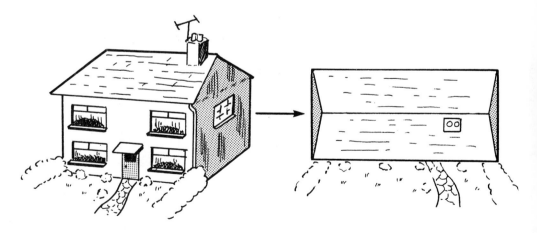

Explain that a map can show where roads lead to and what is beyond the next hill.

2 Using maps

Talk about when maps are used; for example, walking, orienteering, driving, on holiday, finding a particular street on a street plan.

3 Where is our school?

Show the children a street plan of the local area and ask them to find the school on it. How would they describe where it is?

4 Tourist maps

Look at a tourist map (preferably of the local area). These are often given free at Tourist Information Centres. Talk about the various symbols that are used to show features. For example:

information   picnic site   parking

Ask the children to find other symbols on the map and to look at the key to find out what they represent.

5 Splitting up maps

Explain to the children that maps are usually split up into squares so that we can identify features.

6 Showing the position of a square

Talk with the children about how to find positions on a map. The map is split into squares and the lines are numbered. The lines (numbers) going 'east' are eastings, those going 'north' are northings.

We can use a four-figure reference to show a square. For example, the shaded square has the four-figure reference 24 13.

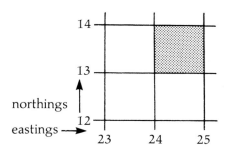

7 Showing the position of a feature

Talk about how we often wish to pinpoint a particular feature or spot rather than just the square it is in. Explain how we think of the sides of the square as being divided into 10 equal divisions. We can use a six-figure reference and say that the building is at 237 124.

Remind the children that to give the eastings first and then the northings.

Draw a large 10 × 10 square on the board and give the children practice in naming six-figure references for particular objects and features.

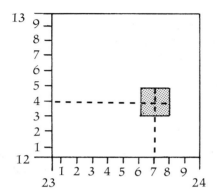

A game to play

SPOT IT

Draw a large grid on the board. Write or hold up a six-figure reference. A child has to come out and mark the spot referred to. This scores a point for his or her team. The turn then passes to the other team. The first team to mark six (or more) correct spots is the winner.

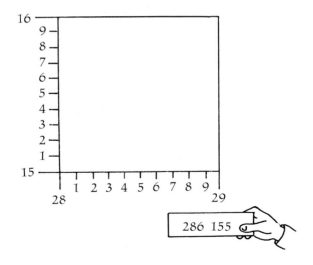

8 Revising scale

Revise the idea of scale, that the actual distance on the ground is represented by a much shorter distance on the map.

Ask what is meant by a 1 cm to 1 metre scale, and a 1 cm to 25 metre scale.

Draw lines for the children to measure and to say what would be their actual distance on the ground. For example:

Scale 1 cm : 25 m

9 Scale on maps

Show the children a variety of maps showing different scales. Explain that the greater the scale, the greater the area that can be shown on the map, but that less detail can then be given.

10 'As the crow flies'

Explain the term 'as the crow flies' is often used when the shortest direct distance is required rather than the distance by road or path.

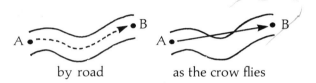

by road   as the crow flies

11 Points of the compass

Revise the eight points of the compass. Show a simple map and ask in what direction you travel to go from one place to another.

LINKS WITH THE ENVIRONMENT

- Look at street and town plans.
- Display a collection of simple route maps, such as safari parks, theme parks and popular walks.
- Display an Ordnance Survey map of the area, showing the location of the school and giving its grid reference.
- Plan a class walk using an Ordnance Survey map.

NOTES ON INVESTIGATIONS

Section A

Do the children realise that a straight edge such as a ruler is not appropriate? They need to use something more flexible, such as a piece of string, and then measure the string against a ruler or against the scale line shown on the pupils' page.

Section B

Check that the children choose sensible scales to show the distance between the telephone and post boxes. There is a relationship between the scales used and the lengths of the lines drawn; when the scale is doubled, the line is halved. For example:

Scale	Length of line
1 cm: 10 m	20 cm
1 cm: 20 m	10 cm
1 cm: 40 m	5 cm

Section C

Do the children check that the scale of the Ordnance Survey map they use is 1 cm: 250 m? This means that 4 cm on the map represents 1 km on the ground so that the walk they plan must be approximately 24 cm on the map. Check that they give correct six-figure grid references and use the eight points of the compass correctly.

Purpose

- To introduce decision trees and how to use them
- To use decision trees to sort and identify

Materials

Reference books about animals may be useful

Vocabulary

Decision tree, identify, database, identity parade, groups, pincers, transparent, data, opposite, descriptions, sort, identity, information

TEACHING POINTS

1 Sorting

Talk with the children about sorting a small number of objects from a collection of buttons, plastic animals or transport sets, logiblocks, three-dimensional shapes, logic people, etc. Point out that it is important to be able to explain how they have been sorted. For example, show the children four two-dimensional shapes from a logiblock set such as:

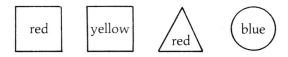

Ask a child to sort them in some way. For example:

squares   not squares

Ask other children to sort them so that each shape is on its own. For example:

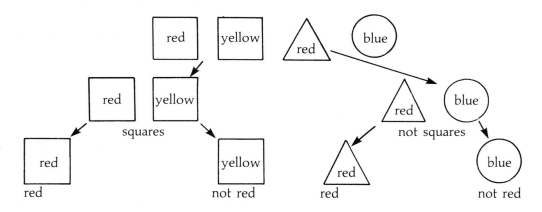

Can any children sort the same shapes in a different way?
   Give the children practice in sorting objects and explaining how they did it.

2 Decision trees

Explain that the sorting activities can be shown on a decision tree. Draw the following decision tree and ask the children to find which number matches these shapes:

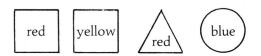

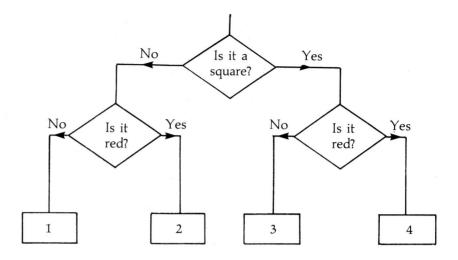

The questions in a decision tree can ask about any property of the shape, such as colour, size or thickness, but they must only be answered 'yes' or 'no'.

Ask the children to draw a decision tree to distinguish between two shapes, for example, a red circle and a blue triangle. Discuss the questions they could use.

Gradually extend the decision tree to three or four objects.

Games to play

FIND THE ANIMAL

Play this game in two teams.

Make a set of cards showing the names and pictures of eight animals. For example:

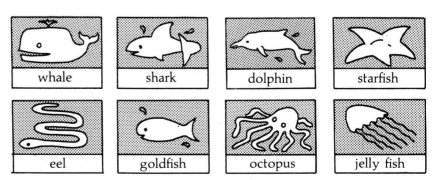

These are placed face upwards in front of both teams.

A player from one team chooses one of the animals and writes it down. This is kept hidden. The children in the second team ask up to four questions to try to name the animal written down. Questions can only be answered 'yes' or 'no'. After four questions,

the children try to guess the animal chosen. If the answer is correct,
1 point is scored. The teams then change over. The first team to
reach 5 points wins the game.

SORT THE ANIMALS

Play this game in two teams.
Draw a blank decision tree:

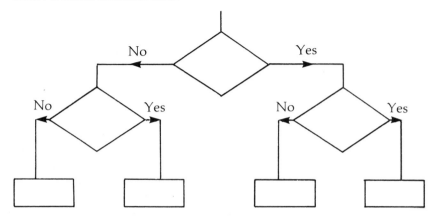

Make sets of four animals cards. For example, one set might be:

dog , cat , robin , sparrow .

Ask the children from the first team to make up questions to sort
the animals and complete the decision tree. For example:

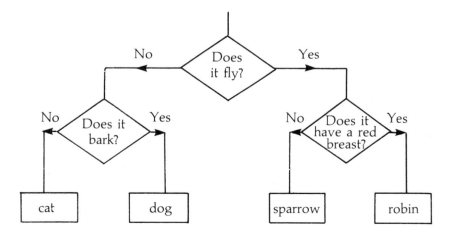

The second team is given four other animals to sort. One point is
scored for each animal correctly sorted. In the example 4 points are
scored.

The game can be extended by one team stating the four animals to sort, the other team finding questions to fit the decision tree.

3 Simple databases

Talk with the children about collecting and entering information in a simple database. Ask the children to complete a record for a database about themselves. For example:

Name	John
Age (years)	10
Sex	male
Height	132 cm
Hair colour	brown
Eye colour	blue

Collect some of the records. Choose one and ask the children to guess who it could be for (give the name last).

Computer databases such as OURFACTS (MESU) and GRASS (Newman College) may be used to enter and access information on a variety of subjects including children, birds, homes, pets, flowers, fruit etc. (See the section on 'Using the computer' earlier in this book.)

4 Punched cards

Explain that some information from simple databases can be put on punched cards. For example:

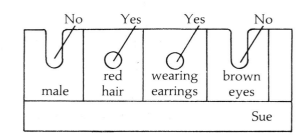

Name	Peter
Sex	Male
Hair colour	brown
Wearing earrings	no
Eye colour	brown

Name	Sue
Sex	Female
Hair colour	red
Wearing earrings	yes
Eye colour	blue

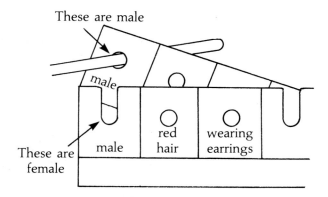

These are male

male

These are female

male   red hair   wearing earrings

Ask some children to transfer information about themselves onto punched cards. The punched cards can then be put together and a knitting needle pushed through the correct hole to answer questions such as:

Who are the people with red hair?
How many males are there?
Who has brown eyes? etc.

Ask the children to write some questions for a friend to find the answer.

LINKS WITH THE ENVIRONMENT

Talk about every day situations which involve sorting and recording data on a database. For example:

- In school – sorting shapes, objects, etc. in mathematics; collecting and identifying leaves, trees, insects, animals in science; keeping registers and records about children and teachers.
- At home – games such as 'Guess Who' involve questions requiring 'yes'/'no' answers.
- Doctor's records – containing information about individuals' health.
- Police – databases on criminals and suspects.
- Banks – records of customers' names, addresses and amounts in their accounts.

NOTES ON INVESTIGATIONS

Section A

Check that the four faces have different features and names, and that the decision tree for the faces is logical and accurate. In particular, are all the answers to the questions 'yes' or 'no'?

Section B

Check that animals with different features are chosen and that the children draw a logical and accurate decision tree, using appropriate questions.

Section C

The children should complete a record for each child in the group. Next, they should draw a logical and accurate decision tree using appropriate questions, but replacing the children's names with a capital letter.

Can other children find the names of the children in the group by using both the database and the decision tree?

Percentages

Purpose

- To recognise and understand simple percentages

Materials

Squared paper, blank hundred squares (for Teacher's resource book activities)

Vocabulary

Percentage, per cent or %, tally chart, table, totals, fraction, tallied, possible percentages

TEACHING POINTS   **1 Percentage – per cent**

Explain that the words 'per cent' mean 'out of 100'. The Latin word *centum* means 'one hundred'. Ask for other words involving 100 which have 'cent' in them; for example, century, centenary, 100 cents = 1 dollar in the USA, 100 centimes = 1 franc in France, etc.

Talk about where percentages are used, for example, marks in tests, inflation, surveys, reductions in price, etc.

Point out that the sign '%' can be used instead of 'per cent'.

2 Colouring percentages

Give each child a blank hundred square and ask them to make a pattern by colouring 16 red squares, 12 blue squares and 20 black.

Point out that 16 out of 100 squares are red, which is $\frac{16}{100}$ or 16%. So 16% of the hundred squares is red.

Do the same for the blue and black squares.

Let the children use two more colours for their pattern, asking them to work out the percentage for each.

Give the children another blank hundred square and ask them to colour in percentages, for example, 4% yellow, 25% purple and so on. Encourage them to explain what they are doing, for example $4\% = \frac{4}{100} = 4$ squares.

Can they tell you anything about 50% or 25%? What about 10% ($\frac{1}{10}$ of all the squares)?

Ask the children to do a supervised traffic count of 100 cars, recording the cars' colours on a blank hundred square. They then work out the percentages for each colour.

A game to play

FIND THE PERCENTAGE

This game is for two groups. Each group needs a large blank hundred square (on 2 cm squared paper) and 100 counters.

Make some percentage cards, for example:

$$\boxed{25\%}, \boxed{12\%}, \boxed{4\%}, \boxed{70\%}.$$

Shuffle the cards and place them face downwards in a pile. Each group in turn takes a card and places a number of counters on their board to match the percentage on the card.

The first group to fill their hundred square with counters wins. (They do not have to get the exact number to finish.)

When all the percentage cards have been used, they can be reshuffled and used again.

3 Practical percentages

Give the children the opportunity to carry out a survey in school.

Ask 100 children if their family takes the old newspapers for recycling. The resulting percentages can be displayed and discussed. They could also do a supervised traffic survey of 100 vehicles to find the percentage of cars, lorries, etc., passing the school.

4 Percentages of 200

Note that this concept is not included in section A.

Talk about how percentages can be used to compare fractions. For example:

$$\frac{100}{200} \rightarrow \frac{50}{100} = 50\%$$

$$\frac{50}{200} \rightarrow \frac{25}{100} = 25\%$$

$$\frac{40}{200} \rightarrow \frac{20}{100} = 20\%$$

Give the children plenty of practice in finding percentages of 200, encouraging them to explain what they are doing.

Talk with them about finding a percentage of 200, for example, 40% of 200. One way to work this out is:

40% of 100 = 40
40% of 200 = 80

Give the children practice and opportunities to discuss their work.

A game to play

MATCHING FRACTIONS

Make pairs of cards showing fractions of 100 and equivalent fractions of 200, for example,

Spread the cards out face downwards on the table. The players take it in turns to pick up two cards. If they are equivalent fractions, the player keeps the pair. If not, the player puts them face down on the table again. The player who collects more pairs in a given time or when all the cards have been used is the winner.

An alternative is to play 'Snap' with the equivalent cards.

5 Percentages of 50

In section C the children are asked to find percentages of 50. They may need to discuss this and to suggest ways of doing it. For example:

10% of 100 = 10, $\frac{1}{10}$ of 100 = 10

so

10% of 50 = 5, $\frac{1}{10}$ of 50 = 5

MENTAL WORK

- Revise halving and doubling numbers, asking questions such as 'If I have 60 stickers and I give half away, how many do I have left?'
  'In a game, I had 40 points but then doubled my score. What did I have then?'
- Revise simple fractions of numbers, for example, $\frac{1}{2}$ of 40, $\frac{1}{4}$ of 80, etc. Again include some verbal problems.
- Ask the children to find $\frac{1}{100}$ of numbers, for example, $\frac{1}{100}$ of 200, 400, 300, etc.
- Ask them equivalence questions, such as

$$\frac{50}{100} = \frac{\square}{2} \qquad \frac{25}{100} = \frac{\square}{4} \qquad \frac{3}{4} = \frac{\square}{100}$$

- Ask them questions on percentages such as:

  'If 7 books out of 100 are picture books, what percentage is this?'
  'What is 17% of 100?'

USING THE CALCULATOR

- Remind the children how to use the constant function on their calculators, asking them to use it to double numbers. For example: 'How many times must you double 2 to reach 1600, 10 to reach 10 000?'
- Give practice in halving numbers. For example: 'Start at 256. How many times do you halve it to reach 1?'
- Give the children practice in finding $\frac{1}{2}$ and $\frac{1}{4}$ of numbers using the calculator.
- Show the children how to use the percentage key on the calculator to convert fractions to percentages. (Note that different calculators may require different key sequences.) They might like to find percentages of 200 using the calculator, for example,

  15% of 200 → 200 × 15 %

A game to play

FIRST TO REACH . . .

Ask the children to keep doubling 2 until they reach 1024. The winner is the first one to tell you how many times they doubled 2.
  Play the game with other numbers.

LINKS WITH THE ENVIRONMENT

- Talk about percentage marks out of 100 in tests and exams.
- Talk about percentages in everyday life: inflation, interest rates, mortgage rates.
- Think about times when we see percentage price reductions, e.g. sales, children's holiday rates in travel brochures.
- Talk about surveys, gallup polls. How many people would be asked?
- Some pie charts show percentages.

NOTES ON INVESTIGATIONS

Section A

Do the children realise that 50% is $\frac{50}{100}$ and that this is the same as $\frac{1}{2}$? Do they suggest other fractions that are equivalent to $\frac{1}{2}$, such as $\frac{2}{4}$, $\frac{3}{6}$, $\frac{4}{8}$, $\frac{5}{10}$, etc?

Section B

Do the children realise that $50\% = \frac{1}{2}$, $25\% = \frac{1}{4}$ and $10\% = \frac{1}{10}$? Do they realise that if their answers are to be whole numbers then the numbers chosen must end in a zero and be divisible by 4, that is, 20, 40, 60, 80? Do they record their findings?

> 50% of 20 = 10
> 25% of 20 = 5
> 10% of 20 = 2

etc.

Section C

Do the children consider 100 birds first, so that 40% of 100 = 40? They may then use a 'halving and doubling' process to maintain an answer of 40. For example:

> 80% of 50 = 40
> 40% of 100 = 40
> 20% of 200 = 40
> 10% of 400 = 40
> 5% of 800 = 40

Discussion might take place as to how the pattern may be extended further.

Number 2

Purpose

- To revise multiplication and division by one digit
- To introduce multiplication of two digits by two digits, and three digits by two digits

Materials

Watch or timer with a second hand, calculators

Vocabulary

Approximately, leap year, divides exactly, average, pulse rate, pulse beat, minutes, hours, days, weeks, months, difference, older, oldest, digit, multiply, largest answer, longer, length, number, per minute, pattern, nearest million, incubation time

TEACHING POINTS   **SECTION A**

1 Multiplication patterns

Remind the children about grouping numbers into 2s, 3s, 4s, 5s, 6s, 7s, 8s, 9s and 10s to make multiplication patterns.

1	2	3	4	5	6	7	8
9	10	11	12	13	14	15	16
17	18	19	20	21	22	23	24
25	26	etc.					

Let them ask their friends questions about the patterns. For example, 'How many eights make 40?'

2 Tables and factors

Revise tables with the children, reminding them of the commutative law and the link between multiplication and division. For example:

$$6 \times 8 = 48 \qquad 48 \div 8 = 6$$
$$8 \times 6 = 48 \qquad 48 \div 6 = 8$$

Ask them about odd and even patterns:

$$\text{odd} \times \text{odd} = \text{odd} \qquad \text{even} \times \text{odd} = \underline{\quad} \qquad \text{even} \times \text{even} = \underline{\quad}$$

Let them continue the pattern into bigger numbers, using their calculators.

Ask puzzle questions such as 'I am thinking of a number. If I multiply it by 2, then 4, the answer is 16. What is the number'?

Remind the children about factors. Ask them to find the factors of 12, 18, 24, etc. and to ring the factors of 30, for example:

Games to play

HOW MANY?

This game is for two or more groups.

Write numbers on the board, for example:

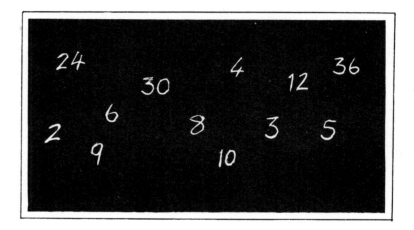

Ask the groups to make as many multiplication sentences as they can, using the numbers. For example:

$6 \times 5 = 30$ or $5 \times 2 \times 3 = 30$

The group which can make the most in a given time is the winner.

FIND THE PATTERN

This game is for two or more groups.

Choose three or four multiplication patterns, for example:

3	6	9	12
4	8	12	16
5	10	15	20

Write them on the board, but jumbled up, and ask the groups to find the patterns. They can only use each number once. The first group to find all the patterns is the winner.

TABLE SNAP

This game can be played by a group of children.

Make a set of cards using multiplication tables and answers so that there are two or more with the same answers. For example:

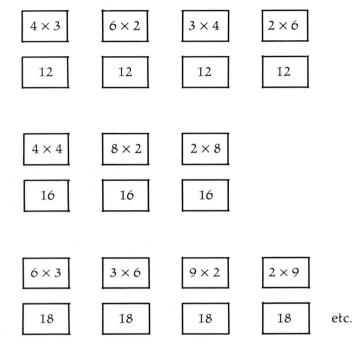

Shuffle and deal them out equally among the players, who play 'Snap' with them. 'Snap' can be called with either 4 × 3 and 12 , or 4 × 3 and 6 × 2 .

3 Multiplication by one digit

Use your own words and methods to revise multiplication by one digit, for example, 242 × 6. Check that the children remember how to 'carry' or exchange. Give them revision practice, encouraging them to use the method they prefer.

Point out that 6(24), for example, means 6 × 24. Give them practice in using brackets in this way.

4 Division by one digit

Revise division by one digit, for example, 435 ÷ 3. Ask the children to suggest different methods and to talk about which one they prefer. Use structural apparatus to give the imagery. Do the children remember how to exchange or 'carry'?

Talk about methods of recording division, for example, $\frac{435}{6}$.

5 Multiplication by 10 and 100

Remind the children about multiplication by 10 and 100, giving them examples, such as 63 × 10 and 63 × 100, to work out on their calculators. What do they notice about the answers?

Can they suggest ways of working them out in their heads? Give them practice in doing this and checking the answers on their calculators.

A game to play

TENS AND HUNDREDS

Two teams and one referee are needed for this game.

Make two sets of cards, one set of four cards:

and another set of 20 cards numbered between 20 and 50.

The referee shuffles both packs and takes one card from the top of each pack, for example:

| 42 | | × 100 |

A player from each team has to write the answer to the problem on the board. The first to do so scores a point for their team. When all the cards in a pack have been used they are reshuffled. The game continues until all the players have had a turn. The winning team is the one with the highest score.

6 Time

Talk with the children about seconds, minutes, hours, days, weeks, years, and their relation to each other. Ask them to work out approximately how many days they had been alive on their last birthday. (Calculators may be necessary.) The answer will be approximate because of leap years.

Talk about leap years and why they occur. There are in fact $365\frac{1}{4}$ days in 1 year as this is how long the earth takes to travel round the sun. It is not practical to have quarter days so the quarters are added to make one extra day in February every fourth year. If the number of the year is exactly divisible by 4 it is a leap year. Look at recent or future years to see which are leap years.

The Olympic Games are held in leap years.

A game to play

LEAP YEARS

This game is for small groups of children.
   Write a selection of year dates on the board:

   1924   1322   1570   1845   1960   1136   etc.

The first group to find all the leap years is the winner.

SECTIONS B AND C

7 Multiplication by 20, 30, 200, 300

Ask the children to suggest ways of multiplying by 20, 30, 40, etc.
Possible methods are

$$
\begin{array}{l}
35 \quad \text{or} \quad 35 \times 20 = 35 \times 2 \times 10 \\
\underline{\times 20} \quad \text{or} \quad 35 \times 10 \times 2
\end{array}
$$

$$35 \times 200 = 35 \times 2 \times 100 \quad \text{or} \quad 35 \times 100 \times 2$$

Can the children think of any others?

8 Multiplication of two digits by two digits

Talk about occasions when this process might be needed. For
example:

   'How many people can be seated at the school concert if there
   are 18 rows of 24 chairs?'

Ask the children to suggest ways of solving this problem, using
pencil and paper methods. Here are some possible methods.

$$
\begin{array}{llll}
24 \times 10 = 240 & 24 & 24 & 24 \\
24 \times \;\; 8 = 192 & \underline{\times \; 18} & \underline{\times \; 18} & \underline{\times \; 18} \\
 \overline{} & 240 \leftarrow 24 \times 10 & 192 \leftarrow 24 \times \;\; 8 & 32 \leftarrow 4 \times \;\; 8 \\
24 \times 18 = 432 & 192 \leftarrow 24 \times \;\; 8 & 240 \leftarrow 24 \times 10 & 160 \leftarrow 20 \times \;\; 8 \\
 \overline{} & \overline{} & \overline{} & 40 \leftarrow 4 \times 10 \\
 & 432 \leftarrow 24 \times 18 & 432 \leftarrow 24 \times 18 & 200 \leftarrow 20 \times 10 \\
 & & & \overline{} \\
 & & & 432 \leftarrow 24 \times 18
\end{array}
$$

They might be interested in another alternative. Draw a rectangle 24 × 18 on squared paper. Divide the 18 into 10 and 8 to make two rectangles. Work out their total area, i.e. the multiplication (24 × 10) + (24 × 8).

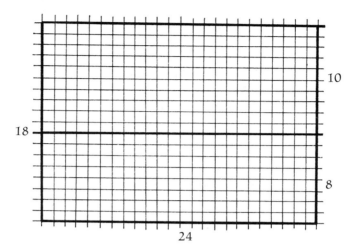

Discuss the children's suggestions and the possible advantages and disadvantages of each one. Give them practice in using their chosen method and recording their work.

9 Multiplication of three digits by two digits

Ask the children to suggest ways of solving 124 × 18. Two possible methods are:

$$
\begin{array}{r}
124 \\
\times \quad 18 \\
\hline
1240\,(\times\,10) \\
992\,(\times\,8) \\
\hline
2232\,(\times\,18)
\end{array}
\qquad
\begin{array}{l}
124 \times 10 = 1240 \\
124 \times 8 = 992 \\
\hline
124 \times 18 \quad 2232
\end{array}
$$

Discuss the children's suggestions and give them practice in using them and recording their work.

10 Further work on time

Talk about how it is sometimes necessary to give approximate answers to problems about time. For example, 52 weeks in a year is actually only 364 days. Similarly, it is difficult to work out the exact number of hours or minutes someone has been alive, since it depends on the time of birth and leap years.

Can the children suggest why the pupils' book only gives the average life span of animals?

11 Millions (introduced in Section C only)

Talk about one million (or one thousand thousands) and how to record it as 1 000 000. What is the biggest number of millions that can be displayed on school calculators?

As a school calculator may only display eight digits, it may be necessary for the children to solve some of the calculations in section C using pencil and paper methods. For this reason it is suggested that the children should round the shrew's heart beat to the nearest million.

MENTAL WORK
- Give the children practice in using tables and factors.
- Ask questions which involve multiplication. For example: 'If there are 16 biscuits in a packet, how many will there be in 9 packets?'
- Give the children practice in multiplying by 10, 20, 30, etc.

A game to play

TOCK

Choose a factor, for example, 4. Ask the children to count in sequence round the class. If their number has a factor of 4 they must say 'Tock' instead of the number. Anyone who makes a mistake is out of the game.

USING THE CALCULATOR
- Ask the children to find factors of bigger numbers such as 72, 96, 132.
- Ask them to multiply bigger numbers by 10, 20, 30, 40, etc. and 100, 200, 300, 400, etc. Encourage them to estimate the answers first.
- Ask the children to explore the different ways of multiplying two digits by two digits, and three digits by two digits.

A game to play

TENS AND HUNDREDS

Children can play this in pairs or small groups. Ask them to display 48 on their calculators and change it to 4800 in two multiplications. The first pair or group to give the answer ($48 \times 10 \times 10 = 4800$) scores a point.

Can they do it in one multiplication?

The level of difficulty of the game can be developed and extended according to the capabilities of the children. For example, change 24 to 4800 using two multiplications.

LINKS WITH THE ENVIRONMENT

Talk about everyday situations involving multiplication.

- Calculating number of available seats in a theatre or concert hall.
- Ordering stock, for example equipment for school, in packs or boxes of 10, 12, 24.
- Buying items such as party gifts and working out the cost, for example, 12 prizes at 35p each.
- Calculating food for parties or other large events, for example, 14 packets of sausage rolls (12 in a packet).

NOTES ON INVESTIGATIONS

Section A

The children need to take their pulse rate first at rest and then after walking, jumping and running. Do they walk, jump and run for the same period of time, for example, 1 minute, to ensure the test is fair, and do they allow their pulse rate to return to normal before each new test? Do they devise a suitable recording chart?

Section B

To obtain the largest possible answer the 9 must be used as the hundreds digit and the 7 and the 5 as the tens digits. The children may use a trial-and-improvement method to arrive at an answer of 69 496. For example:

$$953 \times 72 = 68\,616$$
$$952 \times 73 = 69\,496$$

Section C

$$143 \times 14 = 2002$$
$$143 \times 21 = 3003$$
$$143 \times 28 = 4004$$
$$143 \times 35 = 5005$$
$$143 \times 42 = 6006$$

The pattern increases by $143 \times 7 = 1001$ each time. The pattern can be shown as follows:

$$143 \times 1(7) = 1001$$
$$143 \times 2(7) = 2002$$
$$143 \times 3(7) = 3003 \text{ etc.}$$

Number 3

Purpose

- To revise negative numbers in familiar contexts
- To use negative numbers in context

Materials

Squared paper, thermometer, calculators, geography reference books, newspapers showing world temperatures

Vocabulary

Temperature, thermometer, coldest, hottest, freezing, boiling, below freezing, zero, grid, freezing point, below zero, midnight, range in temperature, storage temperature, negative number, Arctic, Antarctic, temperature difference, comfortable room temperature, symbols, storage time, degrees

TEACHING POINTS   SECTION A

1 Negative numbers

Discuss negative numbers and where they are used in everyday life, for example, when talking about the weather or when they appear on a calculator.

2 Thermometers

Ask the children how temperatures are measured. Show a thermometer and explain how it works. The liquid in it expands as it grows warmer and contracts as it grows colder; this makes it move up or down the tube depending upon the temperature. Many thermometers show the Celsius scale (named after the scientist Celsius (1701–44) who devised the scale). Water boils at 100 °C and freezes at 0 °C. The Celsius scale is sometimes called the centigrade scale because of the 100 graduations between the freezing and boiling points.

Remind the children how to read the temperature on a thermometer. Ask several children to estimate the room temperature. One child can then check it using the thermometer.

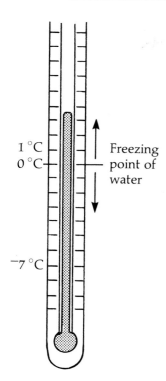

1 °C
0 °C — Freezing
point of
water

⁻7 °C

3 Above and below zero

Draw a thermometer or temperature scale. Mark the freezing point. Remind the children that 'minus 5' means 5 degrees below freezing point which is written ⁻5 °C.

Choose temperatures between 10 °C and ⁻10 °C for individual children to show on the temperature scale. Ask questions like:

Which is colder, ⁻5 °C or ⁻3 °C?
Which is hotter, ⁻7 °C or 1 °C?
How many degrees below zero is ⁻9 °C?

A game to play

HOT, COLD OR FREEZING?

Make a set of 21 temperature cards ranging from 10 °C to ⁻10 °C and a set of nine larger, coloured cards, three of which show 'hottest temperature', three 'coldest temperature' and three 'freezing temperature'.

Ask a group of children to shuffle both sets of cards and place them face down. Each child is dealt one temperature card, then the top coloured card is turned over. Suppose it reads 'coldest temperature'. The child whose temperature card is the coldest, in this case, scores a point. The cards are then reshuffled and dealt out, and a new coloured card is turned over. The winner is the first to score 10 points.

4 Checking the temperature

Encourage the children to check the temperature outside at a fixed time each day and keep a record. The data could be put onto a computer database.

A graph or chart might be kept of the temperatures of different cities around the world, often shown in newspapers.

SECTIONS B AND C

5 Temperature range

Talk with the children about how temperatures change during the day and ask them to keep a record for one day. Draw a thermometer and mark on it the highest and lowest temperatures they find. Explain that the difference between the highest and lowest temperature is the range, i.e. the range between 2 °C and

⁻2 °C is 4 degrees. Choose different temperatures for highest and lowest and ask the children to use the thermometer to find the range.

Note: work of this kind is included in the pupils' book.

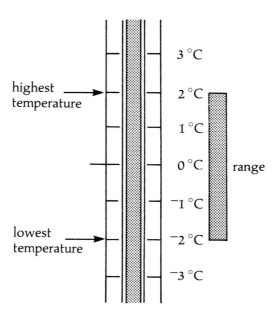

6 Lifts

Use the context of a lift in a department store or block of flats to develop work on negative numbers. Remember to include the basements. Ask the children to work out the number of floors the lift travels between different levels. For example, from the basement (⁻1) to the third floor (3) is 4 floors. This could be recorded:

$$- 1 \text{ to } +3 \rightarrow 4 \text{ floors}$$

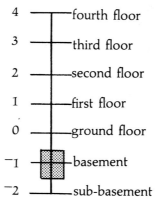

7 Underwater

The context of negative numbers could be linked to underwater movement of a diving bell.

Ask the children how many fathoms (a fathom is 6 feet) the diving bell has travelled if it is moved to different levels.

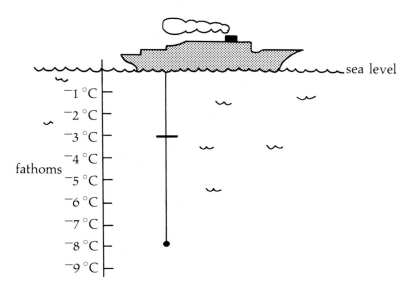

8 Number lines

Use the number line as a context for negative numbers. This could be chalked on the floor.

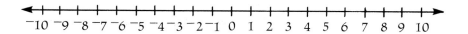

Ask a child to stand at a starting number on the line and step forwards or backwards to reach a finishing number. For example:

> Stand on ⁻6. How many numbers do you step on to reach 4?
> (10)
> Start on 7. How many numbers do you step on to reach ⁻5?
> (12)

A game to play

FIND THE DISTANCE

Play this game in two teams. Use the number line and a stop watch. Make a set of number cards from ⁻10 to 10 and shuffle them.

Ask a player from the first team to draw two number cards, for example, $\boxed{\ ^-6\ }$, $\boxed{\ 8\ }$. A player from the second team must find the number of spaces between the two numbers on the number line in a specified time (such as 15 seconds). The teams then change over and the cards are reshuffled. Each correct answer scores a point. The winning team is the first to reach 10 points.

MENTAL WORK   Ask the children questions involving negative numbers.

- How many degrees below zero is $^-6\,^{\circ}$C?
- What are the next two numbers in these patterns?

8, 6, 4, 2, 0, $^-2$, □, □
$^-11$, $^-8$, $^-5$, □, □

- Which is colder, $^-6\,^{\circ}$C or $^-4\,^{\circ}$C?
- What is the range in temperature between 2 $^{\circ}$C and $^-3\,^{\circ}$C?
- If the temperature was 2 $^{\circ}$C and dropped 4 degrees, what is the temperature now?

USING THE   Ask the children to count back in ones from 8 to $^-8$ using the
CALCULATOR   constant function. Talk about what happens. Repeat the activity counting back in 2s. Choose different starting and finishing numbers. Try counting on in 3s using the constant function from $^-15$ to 0 – how many presses are needed?

LINKS WITH THE   Talk about everyday situations where negative numbers and
ENVIRONMENT   temperatures are used.

- Frozen foods are stored at temperatures below zero.
- Ice lollies are often made at home. What temperatures are required?
- TV weather forecasts often show temperatures below freezing.
- Look at and keep a chart of daily temperatures both locally and in other parts of the world.

NOTES ON   **Section A**
INVESTIGATIONS
The children should make up different symbols appropriate for a television weather map, including some symbols for negative temperatures. Do they show an appropriate temperature to match each symbol? For example:

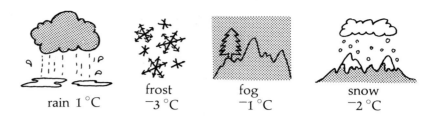

rain 1 °C   frost $^-3$ °C   fog $^-1$ °C   snow $^-2$ °C

Section B

Different combinations of negative numbers can be used to get $^-6$.
For example:

$$^-1-5=^-6 \qquad ^-5-1=^-6$$
$$^-2-4=^-6 \qquad ^-4-2=^-6$$
$$^-3-3=^-6$$

Some children may use zero to reach $^-6$:

$$0-6=^-6 \quad \text{or} \quad ^-6-0=^-6$$

Addition may also be used, for example, $^-7+1=^-6$.

Section C

The children's suggestions could include any of the following:
proximity to the equator, cloud cover (e.g. desert lands), height
above sea level, the direction of winds (e.g. colder from Siberia),
distance inland.

Data 2

Purpose

- To revise the reading, construction and interpretation of
  pictograms, block graphs, bar-line graphs and frequency charts
- To revise grouping data into equal class intervals
- To design and use an observation sheet to collect data, collate
  and analyse results
- To construct and interpret pie charts
- To introduce scatter graphs and to interpret them

Materials

Squared paper, clock stamp

Vocabulary

Block graph, survey, data, mean, average, total, labels, tally, frequency chart, age grouping, bar chart, pie chart, fraction, midnight, noon, most frequent, stride length, scatter graph, reach, bar-line graph, represents

TEACHING POINTS   **SECTION A**

1 Data

Talk about the word 'data', reminding the children that graphs are often used to show collected data. Ask them to suggest what information could be collected about themselves; ideas might include hair colour, eye colour, favourite TV programmes, sports, etc.

Ask them to design a data collection sheet for their favourite drinks. Tallying is one way of collecting data. For example:

	Tally	Total
orange	̶H̶H̶					9
vimto	̶H̶H̶	5
coke	̶H̶H̶ ̶H̶H̶	10
lemonade	̶H̶H̶			7
milk					3
water			1

2 Drawing and interpreting graphs

Ask the children to draw a graph to show the data, first discussing the different graphs that could be drawn. For example:

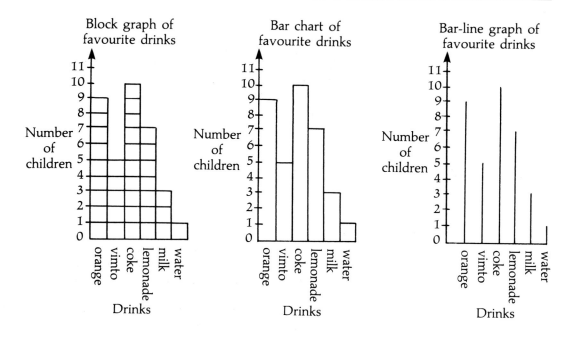

Remind them about the importance of labelling the axes, a title and correct numbering.

Encourage the children to interpret their graphs by asking them questions. Alternatively, the children could ask each other questions. Ask some children to describe their graph orally or in writing.

Remind them that bar-line graphs can be drawn horizontally. For example:

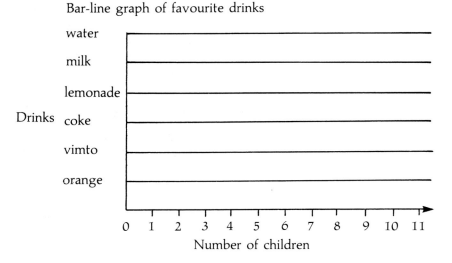

Ask whether it makes sense to join the ends of the bar-line graph with straight lines. In this case it does not make sense because the drinks are separate or discrete items.

3 Frequency charts

Revise the word 'frequency' and explain that a bar chart with an axis showing frequency can be called a 'frequency chart' or 'frequency diagram'.

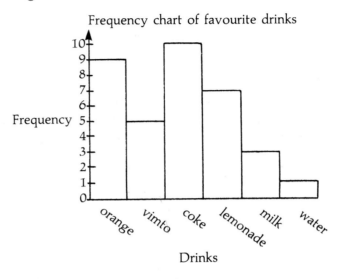

4 Scale

Remind the children to use appropriate scales when drawing graphs. For example:

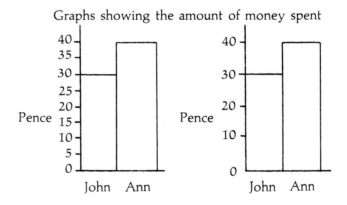

Ask the children to suggest a scale for drawing a graph to show the height in centimetres of 10 children in the class, or the number of seconds it takes to complete a task.

5 Grouped data

Draw a frequency chart showing grouped data. For example:

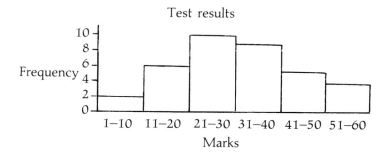

Test results

Ask questions about the chart. For example:

How many children scored between 31 and 40 marks?
What was the most frequent mark group scored in the test?
How many children did the test?
How many children got less than 21 marks?

Remind the children that groupings must be equal sized. Draw different grouping tables for the children to complete. For example:

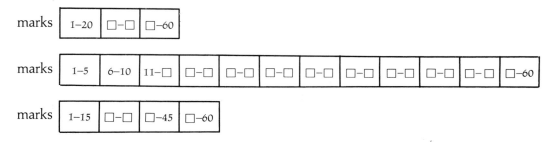

A game to play

EQUAL GROUPING

Play this game in two teams. Make a set of number cards, for example, 12, 18, 20, 24, 30, 32, 36, 40, 48. Shuffle the cards. The first team turns over the top card, for example 20, and has to draw as many different equal grouping tables for it as they can. For example:

1–5	6–10	11–15	16–20

1–4	5–8	9–12	13–16	17–20

Each correct table scores a point.
The teams then change over. The team with the most points after an equal number of turns is the winner.

6 Symbols to represent a group of units

Remind the children that sometimes symbols are used to represent numbers. Ask them to interpret the following table showing the results of a survey about how a class of children travel to school. Check that they understand how ◁, ◁▷ and ⊕ show 1, 2 and 3 children.

walk	⊕ ⊕ ⊕ ⊕	16
bus	⊕ ◁	5
car	⊕ ⊕ ◔	11
bicycle	◁▷	2

⊕ represents 4 children

Other symbols could be used, such as ▯.

SECTION B

7 Introduce pie charts

Introduce pie charts by explaining that a pie is often divided into different fractions at meal times; in mathematics a pie chart is a circle divided into fractions.
    Draw some pie charts, asking the children what fraction they have been divided into.

8 Interpreting pie charts

Draw different pie charts and ask the children appropriate questions in order to check that they can interpret them.

This pie chart represents 20 people.
How many are adults?
How many are girls?
How many are boys?

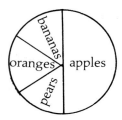

This pie chart shows the favourite fruit of 12 children.
How many children preferred apples?
What fraction of the pie chart shows pears?
How many children preferred pears?
How many children preferred bananas?
How many children preferred oranges?

Draw a pie chart. Give the children some information and ask them questions about it. For example:

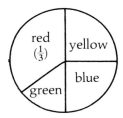

12 people like red best.
How many people preferred yellow?
How many preferred green?
How many people does the pie chart show altogether?

9 Drawing simple pie charts

Fold a paper circle into eighths. This can be used as a template to draw a pie chart showing that there are 5 girls in a group of 8 children, for example.

A clock stamp which divides the circle into twelfths is used in the pupils' book.

10 Harder pie charts

Explain that angles need to be calculated and drawn accurately for some pie charts. Ask them to draw a pie chart for the following data about the favourite subjects of a class of children.

9	English
12	Mathematics
9	Science
6	Art
36	

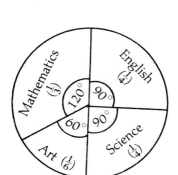

Talk about how the children worked out the angles. Two possible methods are:

Method 1
(using fractions of 36)

English	$\frac{9}{36} \rightarrow \frac{1}{4} \rightarrow 90°$	
Mathematics	$\frac{12}{36} \rightarrow \frac{1}{3} \rightarrow 120°$	
Science	$\frac{9}{36} \rightarrow \frac{1}{4} \rightarrow 90°$	
Art	$\frac{6}{36} \rightarrow \frac{1}{6} \rightarrow 60°$	

Method 2
(using fractions of 360°, i.e. $\frac{360}{36} = 10°$)

English	$9 \times 10° \rightarrow 90°$
Mathematics	$12 \times 10° \rightarrow 120°$
Science	$9 \times 10° \rightarrow 90°$
Art	$6 \times 10° \rightarrow 60°$

Let the children decide which method is appropriate for each question. For example, ask them to draw a pie chart to show that, in a box of chocolates, 7 were nuts, 8 were creams and 5 were caramels – method 2 is probably more appropriate in this case.

SECTION C

11 Scatter graphs

Explain that scatter graphs can be used to show two different aspects of collected data.

Draw a scatter graph showing data about the height and arm length of a group of children. Explain that each cross represents one child. Ask:

How many children does the scatter graph show?
How many children have an arm length of 56 cm?
How many children are 144 cm tall?

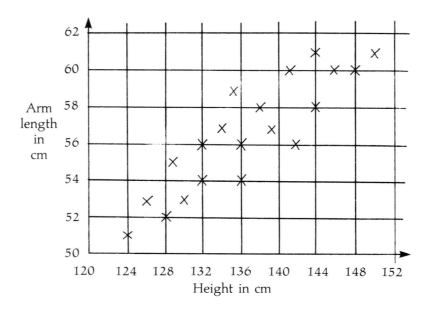

12 Continuous scatter graphs

Talk about whether there is a relationship between height and arm length; that is, what can you say about the arm length of taller children?

Some scatter graphs may show a positive correlation or relationship. For example, the arm length of taller children tends to be longer. (Note: the 'line of best fit' on a scatter graph is not required at National Curriculum Level 6.)

Features such as height, weight, stride, age, arm length, reach are continuous, so the scatter graph for these aspects is a continuous one.

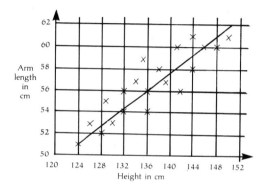

13 Discrete scatter graphs

Scatter graphs can also be drawn about data which is exact, such as girl/boy, birthday month, pets, number of brothers/sisters, eye colour, hair colour, etc. Because the data is about unrelated or separate features, this kind of graph is called a discrete scatter graph. For example, the scatter graph showing the numbers of brothers and sisters for each child is discrete. Ask:

How many children does the scatter graph show?
How many children have 2 brothers and 1 sister? (2)
How many have no brothers or sisters? (3)

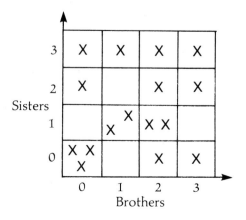

Explain that because the data is about discrete or separate items, there is no relationship between the numbers of brothers and sisters a particular child has.

Computer programs such as OURFACTS and GRASS (see the section on 'Using the computer' earlier in this book) can be used to collect data and display it as scatter graphs.

LINKS WITH THE ENVIRONMENT

Talk about everyday situations where data is displayed and where results or scores can be grouped equally.

- Newspapers and magazines showing statistics – graphs, pie charts, grouped data from opinion polls.
- Geography – graphs showing products of countries, population.
- Sport – recording scores, using equal group intervals.
- School – grouping scores to show patterns of achievement.

NOTES ON INVESTIGATIONS

Section A

Check that the children list a variety of activities for their chosen day and that they round the times to the nearest hour. Do they check that the times total 24 hours? Their graphs should show the data clearly. Are their questions about the graph relevant and appropriate for other children?

Section B

Do the children design an appropriate data collection sheet to collect the data? Do they choose children of the same age for their investigations? Do they group the heights in equal intervals? Do the children come to any conclusion about whether boys or girls of the same age in the class are taller? Are their explanations supported by the data collected?

Section C

Check that the children choose characteristics that can be appropriately shown as a scatter graph, height and stride, or height and weight. Do they design and use an appropriate data collection sheet? Does the scatter graph show the data accurately? Do the children conclude that there is some relationship between the characteristics chosen? Do the children's explanations indicate that they understand scatter graphs?

Probability 2

Purpose

- To revise likelihood of events
- To understand and use the probability scale from 0 to 1
- To list possible outcomes of events
- To give and justify subjective estimates of probabilities
- To use notation for the probability of equally likely events, for example, $\frac{1}{n}$ for one of n events
- To introduce estimates of probability based on statistical evidence

Materials

Cubes (yellow and blue), small bags (not transparent), counters, counters with 0 on one side and X on the other, dice, reels (red, blue and yellow), pots, pack of playing cards

Vocabulary

Chance, even chance, certain, tally, total, fair game, probability, tally charts, predict, record, several, random, forward, design, experiment

TEACHING POINTS   SECTION A

1 Outcome of events

Talk with the children about how there can be different outcomes or results of events. For example, what might be the results of a netball match? The team could win, lose or draw.

Ask what might be the outcome of tossing a coin. Have head and tail an even chance of being thrown? Let the children toss a coin 20 times, make a tally of the results and discuss them.

When throwing a die, is there an equal chance of getting an odd number? Is there an even chance, or less than even chance, of getting a 6? Let the children tally the results of 60 throws of a die. Discuss the outcomes.

2 Revise likelihood

Remind the children about describing the likelihood of events as 'very likely', 'likely', 'unlikely' or 'very unlikely'. Ask them to write a statement such as 'I shall go swimming tomorrow' and decide which of the descriptions fits best. Would their choice of 'very likely', for example, be the same for everyone?

3 Using the probability scale from 0 to 1

Draw a probability scale.

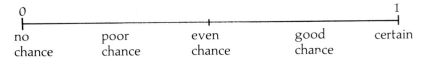

Ask the children to write three statements and decide where each would fit on the probability scale. Discuss statements which have no chance and those which are certain. Point out that the numerical values 0 and 1 respectively are assigned to these. For example, 'All the oceans in the world will dry up tomorrow' has no chance of happening, a probability of 0. 'It will be 3 o'clock sometime tomorrow' is certain, a probability of 1.

Work on the probability scale is included in the pupils' book.

A game to play

DECIDE

Play this game in two teams.

Make some statement cards. For example:

| It will rain tomorrow | | The sun will shine tomorrow |

Draw a probability scale from 0 to 1 on the board. Share the statements out between the teams and give them time to discuss where each should fit on the probability scale. The first team positions one statement on the line. The other team discusses the placing. If they agree and the teacher agrees the placing, the first team scores a point. The teams then change over. The winner is the first team to score 5 points.

4 Listing possible outcomes

Talk about the possible outcomes when tossing a coin (H or T). Ask the children to record all the possible outcomes when throwing two coins together. For example:

1st coin	2nd coin
H	H
H	T
T	H
T	T

Ask them to list all possible outcomes when throwing a die (1, 2, 3, 4, 5, 6). Can they list the different ways of scoring 7 using two dice?

1 + 6	4 + 3
2 + 5	5 + 2
3 + 4	6 + 1

Can they list all the ways of scoring other totals, such as 10 or 6? Two dice of different sizes or colours could be used to distinguish 5 + 2 from 2 + 5.

Ask them to list all possible outcomes when taking two marbles from a pot containing equal numbers of coloured marbles, for example 6 red, 6 blue – RR RB BR BB.

5 Estimates of probabilities

Ask the children to make sensible estimates of probability. For example, ask what is the chance of getting an even number when throwing a die. Do they say the probability is '3 out of 6', or '1 out of 2' or $\frac{1}{2}$? Similarly, when a fair coin is tossed, ask what is the probability of getting a tail. Discuss these in relation to the probability scale which shows $\frac{1}{2}$.

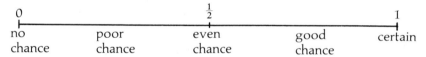

Talk about statements which might have probability $\frac{1}{2}$, such as, 'what is the chance of it being sunny today?'

Games to play

WHAT'S THE CHANCE?

Play this game in two teams.
Make a set of number cards from
1 to 10 and a set of chance cards.

		will not divide by 2
odd	even	will divide by 2
more than 5	less than 6	part of 2s table
part of 3s table	six	ten

Both sets of cards are shuffled. Each team starts with 3 points. A child from the first team turns over a chance card, for example even, and then must decide whether to take a chance and turn over a number card or pass it to the opposing team to turn over. If the number card is turned over and it is correct (i.e. is even in this case) 2 points are scored. If it is incorrect (i.e. not even), 1 point is deducted from the score. The turn then passes to the second team. The winner is the first to reach 11 points or when the opponents reach zero.

The game could be adapted by using picture cards of plane shapes such as 6 triangles, 10 squares, 4 circles, and 20 name cards triangle, square, circle. A name card is turned over first and a child decides whether to turn over a shape card or pass it to the opponent. It is important that the children know the proportion of shape cards when making the decision whether to turn over or pass it on.

CHANCE THE DOMINO

Use a set of dominoes or make a set from card. Make about 20 statement cards such as adds up to 7, less than 4, etc., and shuffle them. Each player starts with 3 points. The first player turns over a card and then must decide whether to turn over a domino or pass it to the opponent to turn over. If the spots on the domino match the words on the card (for example, the domino on the left adds up to 7), 2 points are scored by the player turning over the domino. If it is incorrect (i.e. does not add up to 7), 1 point is deducted from their score. The turn then passes to the second player. The winner is the first to reach 11 points or when an opponent reaches zero.

SECTIONS B AND C

6 Surveys

Ask the children to make a survey to record the colour of cars passing the school. Ask them to design a data collection sheet.

	Number of cars	Total
red	⊬⊬⊬ III	8
blue	⊬⊬⊬ ⊬⊬⊬ II	12
green	III	3
yellow	⊬⊬⊬ I	6
white	⊬⊬⊬ IIII	9

Discuss the results of the survey and ask the children to estimate the most likely colour of car to pass the school next. What is the least likely colour?

Similar surveys could be carried out by collecting data about cars being driven by women, or being British, or a survey of the types of birds visiting a bird table.

Discuss the findings and ask the children to give estimates of the probability of the next event on the basis of their findings.

7 Repeating activities and outcomes

Ask different groups of children to toss a coin 10 times and tally the results. Does everyone get the same results? Why not?

This type of activity could be carried out with spinners. Do the children appreciate that if an activity is repeated, different outcomes may result?

8 Notation

Talk with the children about the probability of drawing a blue marble from a pot containing one blue and one green marble. (Beads or cubes could also be used.) Has each marble an equal chance of being drawn out? Explain that we can record the probability of drawing the blue marble as '1 out of 2' or $\frac{1}{2}$. Similarly, if three different coloured marbles are placed in a pot the probability of drawing one particular coloured marble is '1 out of 3' or $\frac{1}{3}$.

This work is developed in the pupils' book.

9 Sampling

Use a sample bottle or a pot containing the same number of red and blue beads (for example, 4 red, 4 blue). Tell the children the number of beads it contains but not the proportion. Ask them to withdraw one bead at a time and record the colour before replacing it. Do this 40 times. Can the children predict the proportions from their results? For example:

sample bottle

8 beads

red bead

	Tally		rounds to
red	╫╫ ╫╫ ╫╫ ╫╫ I	21	21→20
blue	╫╫ ╫╫ ╫╫ IIII	19	19→20

Prediction: About the same number of red and blue beads (i.e. if 8 beads, 4 red, 4 blue). The predicted probability of drawing a particular colour bead would then be written as $\frac{1}{2}$ for a red bead, $\frac{1}{2}$ for a blue.

Ask the children to repeat this activity using different proportions of coloured beads (for example, 2 red, 6 blue). Can the children predict the proportions and record the probability?

This work is developed in the pupils' book.

10 Combining events

Talk about ways of recording the probabilities of combined events such as listing all the possible outcomes when tossing two coins.

First coin	Second coin	Probability
H	H →	$\frac{1}{4}$
H	T $\rbrace$ →	$\frac{2}{4}$
T	H	
T	T →	$\frac{1}{4}$

Probability

$$H \Big\langle \begin{array}{l} H \quad (HH) \to \frac{1}{4} \\ T \quad (HT) \end{array}$$
$$T \Big\langle \begin{array}{l} H \quad (TH) \end{array} \Big\rbrace \to \frac{2}{4}$$
$$\qquad T \quad (TT) \to \frac{1}{4}$$

Similarly, the results of throwing two counters, each with one side marked 1 and the other marked 2, might be recorded as:

1st	2nd	Probability
1	1 →	$\frac{1}{4}$
1	2 $\rbrace$ →	$\frac{2}{4}$
2	1	
2	2 →	$\frac{1}{4}$

+	1	2
1	2	3
2	3	4

$Pr(2) \to \frac{1}{4}$
$Pr(3) \to \frac{2}{4}$
$Pr(4) \to \frac{1}{4}$

In this example the probability of scoring 2 is $Pr(2) \to \frac{1}{4}$.

Ask the children to throw two dice and record the totals. This can be shown as an addition table. Can they work out the theoretical probabilities from it?

+	1	2	3	4	5	6
1	2	3	4	5	6	7
2	3	4	5	6	7	8
3	4	5	6	7	8	9
4	5	6	7	8	9	10
5	6	7	8	9	10	11
6	7	8	9	10	11	12

$Pr(2) \rightarrow \frac{1}{36}$ $Pr(7) \rightarrow \frac{6}{36}$

$Pr(3) \rightarrow \frac{2}{36}$ $Pr(8) \rightarrow \frac{5}{36}$

$Pr(4) \rightarrow \frac{3}{36}$ $Pr(9) \rightarrow \frac{4}{36}$

$Pr(5) \rightarrow \frac{4}{36}$ $Pr(10) \rightarrow \frac{3}{36}$

$Pr(6) \rightarrow \frac{5}{36}$ $Pr(11) \rightarrow \frac{2}{36}$

$Pr(12) \rightarrow \frac{1}{36}$

In this example the probability of scoring 2 is $Pr(2) \rightarrow \frac{1}{36}$. Ask what is the probability of scoring a total of 1 (no chance, so $Pr(1) \rightarrow 0$).

A game to play

TOTALS

The children play in pairs. They throw two dice and add the totals. One child gains a point for each total of 6 or less, the other a point for each total of 7 or more. Ask the children to play for 36 throws of the dice, keeping a running total of their scores. Which child is winning? (From the table, the probability of a total of 6 or less is $\frac{15}{36}$, and that of 7 or more is $\frac{21}{36}$).

Is it a fair game? Why not? How could they make it a 'fair' game? (For example, no one scores when the dice add up to 7.)

11 Recording events

Show the children the quincunx or binostat (if available). Explain that these work by a ball passing to either side of a peg; the ball has an equal chance of going to either side.

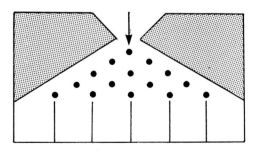

Talk with the children about recording the theoretical probability of various events. For example:

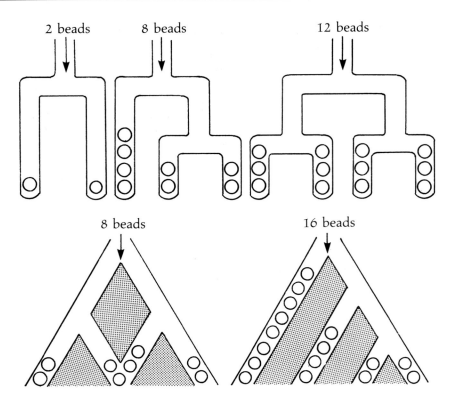

2 beads   8 beads   12 beads

8 beads   16 beads

Can the children devise their own diagrams to show theoretical probabilities of events?

MENTAL WORK   Ask the children to work out mentally the probability of various events. For example:

- What is the probability of drawing the following cards from a pack of 52 playing cards?
    (a)   a black card
    (b)   a heart
    (c)   an ace
    (d)   a red queen
    (e)   not a club
- What is the probability of throwing a six-sided die and the following happening?
    (a)   a 4
    (b)   an even number
    (c)   a multiple of 3
    (d)   not a 6
    (e)   not the number which came up the previous time
- What is the probability of drawing the following from a pot containing 3 red beads and 1 blue bead?
    (a)   a red bead
    (b)   a blue bead

LINKS WITH THE ENVIRONMENT

Talk about everyday situations involving probability.

- Board games use dice or spinners to give fairness.
- Sports events – tossing up at the beginning to choose ends or who starts. In sports like tennis, racquets are spun to choose ends.
- Raffles – prize draws rely on fairness. Tickets are often drawn from a drum.
- Draws – Premium Bonds, cup draws for sports events.
- Bingo games often use numbered table tennis balls. These are usually chosen by being sucked up a tube.

NOTES ON INVESTIGATIONS

Section A

Do the children design an appropriate board for their game, which should also use two dice and two counters? Are the rules clear and logical? Is it a fair game? Do the children explain their game clearly?

Section B

A suitable data collection sheet might be:

	Tally	Total
red red		
red blue or blue red		
blue blue		

The children will probably find that one red reel and one blue reel is the most frequent combination pulled out. Can they explain why this should happen? (After pulling out one red reel there are 2 out of 3 chances of pulling out a blue reel.) Do the children appreciate that although it is possible to get no red reels in five attempts, it is extremely unlikely?

Section C

Suppose the children include 3 red cards when choosing 10 cards from a pack of playing cards. Then the probability of drawing a red card is '3 out of 10' or $\frac{3}{10}$ and that of not drawing a red card is $(10-3=)$ '7 out of 10' or $\frac{7}{10}$.

The probability of drawing a particular card from the 10 cards is '1 out of 10' or $\frac{1}{10}$, and the probability of not drawing it is '9 out of 10' or $\frac{9}{10}$.

Do the children notice that the probabilities of each pair adds up to 1?

$$\frac{1}{10} + \frac{9}{10} = \frac{10}{10} = 1$$
$$\frac{3}{10} + \frac{7}{10} = \frac{10}{10} = 1$$

Angles 1

Purpose

- To revise the language associated with angles
- To revise the measurement of angles to 5°
- To introduce congruence of simple shapes
- To introduce angle properties associated with intersecting and parallel lines
- To introduce bearings

Materials

Angle measurers or protractors, rulers, templates of different quadrilaterals, tracing paper, circular protractors

Vocabulary

Angle, measures, protractor, angle measurer, reflex, acute, obtuse, straight, quadrilateral, sum of the angles, predict, prediction, triangle, parallel, equal, pairs of angles, shape, congruent, templates, silhouette, bearing, clockwise angle, north, digits, circular protractor, scale measurements, compass

TEACHING POINTS   SECTION A

1 Angle families

Remind the children about acute, obtuse, straight and reflex angles, and full turns. Let them help you to make a chart:

Acute angles   — between 0° and 90°
Right angles   — 90°
Obtuse angles — between 90° and 180°
Straight angle — 180°
Reflex angle   — between 180° and 360°
Full turn   — 360°

Let them make and name the types of angles with geostrips, open scissors, two strips of card and a paper fastener, or maybe a fan.

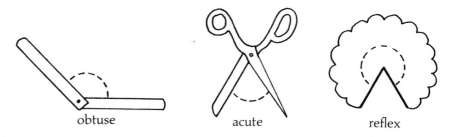

obtuse   acute   reflex

Give the children practice in drawing all the types of angles. Remind them to mark the angles clearly, particularly the reflex ones.

Which of the angles can they find in the classroom? Let them investigate the types of angles on regular plane shapes, e.g. hexagon, pentagon.

Ask them to design a machine or spacecraft using all the types of angle and marking them

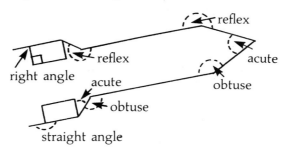

A game to play

ODD ANGLE OUT

This game is for a group of three or four children.
Make a set of 25 cards with an angle drawn on each one

8 acute angles
8 obtuse angles
8 reflex angles
1 right angle

etc.

The cards are shuffled and dealt out. One player has an extra card. The idea is for each player to collect pairs of the same type of angle and to not be left with the right angle card in their hand at the end. Each player looks at their cards and places any pairs of acute, obtuse or reflex angles face upwards on the table in front of them. The player with the extra card then offers their hand for the next player on the left to choose a card (without looking at the faces of the cards). The second player then puts down another pair of angles if they can before offering their hand to the next player. The game continues until all the cards are paired and placed face upwards on the table. The player left with the right angle card is the loser.

2 Measuring angles in 5° and 10°

Remind the children how to measure angles in degrees using a protractor or angle measurer and that the symbol for degrees is °. Check that they remember how many degrees there are in a right angle, a half right angle, a straight angle and a full turn, 2 right angles and 4 right angles. Give them plenty of practice in drawing and measuring angles to 5° and 10°. Duplicate shapes for them to measure the angles.

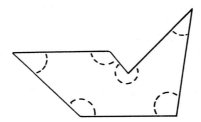

Ask them to use their circular protractors to draw a circle and put marks round the circumference at 30° intervals. They can then join the marks in different ways to make patterns. Talk about these patterns, and devise other circle patterns with different numbers of points around the circle. Can they work out what the angles should be? For example:

8 points → 360°/8 = 45°

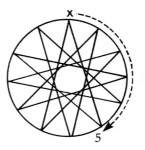

Count round in 5s

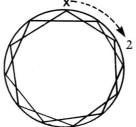

Count round in 2s

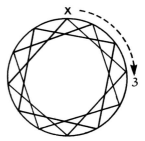

Count round in 3s

3 Estimating angles

Give the children practice in estimating angle sizes before measuring them.

A game to play

ESTIMATE THE ANGLE

This game is for small groups of children.

Draw a set of angles measured to 5° and duplicate a copy for each group. Ask each group to estimate the angles. They can then measure them and compare the true measurements with their estimates. They score

- 3 points for each accurate estimate
- 2 points for an estimate of 5° either side of the true measurement
- 1 point for an estimate of 10° either side of the true measurement

The group with the highest score wins.

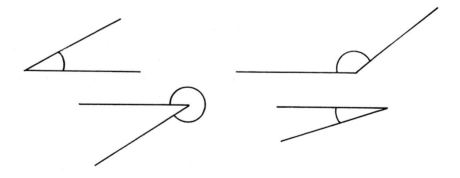

SECTIONS B AND C

4 Congruent shapes

Talk about congruent shapes being identical in shape and size. Make a pair of identical equilateral triangles from card and show the children by fitting one on top of the other that they are the same shape and size.

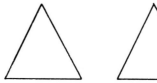

Make an identical pair of right angled triangles and put them on the board in this position, for example.

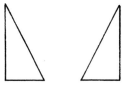

Can the children suggest a way of showing that these are also congruent – by turning one over so that they fit exactly on top of each other?

Let the children find other pairs of congruent plane shapes.

5 Using tracing paper to find congruent shapes

Talk with the children about the difficulties of finding congruent shapes when they are drawn and cannot be physically lifted and fitted on top of each other. Give them practice in tracing a shape and then fitting this on to another shape to see if they are congruent. Remind them that they can turn the tracing round or over.

6 Angles of the triangle and straight angles

Do the children remember that the sum of the angles of any triangle is 180°? If not, ask them to draw and cut out a paper triangle. Then ask them to tear off each corner and to fit the corners together at a centre point. Do they understand that they have made a straight angle of 180°?

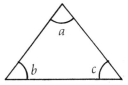   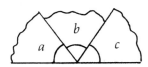

7 Parallel lines

Revise the properties of parallel lines: they are the same distance apart for the whole of their length, and they can be different lengths. Point out that we can use arrows to show lines are parallel.

8 Intersecting lines

Explain that when lines or curves cross or touch, we say they intersect. Look at objects in the school which contain intersecting lines such as window frames, floor tiles, wall bars in PE. Look at maps or plans to see where roads or paths intersect.

Ask the children to draw sets of intersecting parallel lines, using squared paper or isometric paper for accuracy. Can they recognise and name any of the shapes they have made in their patterns?

A game to play

INTERSECT

This game is for two or more children.

Make a simple board game on 2 cm squared paper. (The size is optional.) Mark coloured intersecting lines on the paper.

1	2	3	4	5	6
12	11	10	9	8	7
13	14	15	16	17	18
24	23	22	21	20	19

The children need counters and a die. Each player throws the die and moves their counter along the board accordingly. If they land on a square with a coloured intersection they move back one place (or they miss a turn). The winner is the first player to reach the last square (24 in this case).

9 Angle properties

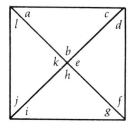

Talk about the angle properties of various shapes. Draw a square, rectangle, parallelogram, rhombus, kite, equilateral triangle, isosceles triangle, scalene triangle and a right angled triangle on the board or display chart. Ask the children to name each one and to tell you anything they notice about its angles.

Draw a large square on a piece of paper, mark the diagonals and label each angle. Ask the children to measure the angles. What do they notice about the angles and the four triangles? (They are congruent and isosceles triangles.)

10 Language

Introduce the language associated with angles, and intersecting and parallel lines if you feel the children can cope with it.

Supplementary angles add up to 180°.

Complementary angles add up to 90°.

Vertically opposite angles

Alternate angles

Corresponding angles

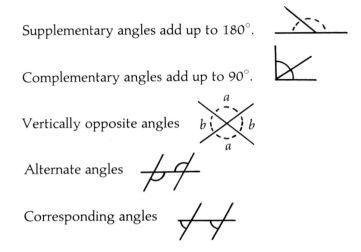

If the associated language will confuse the children at this stage, just give them practice in looking for relationships between angles, particularly when made by intersecting and parallel lines.

11 Sherlock Holmes

It might be useful to talk to the children about Conan Doyle's Sherlock Holmes, Dr Watson, Baker Street, 'The Hound of the Baskervilles', etc. in preparation for work on this chapter.

12 Bearings

Revise the points of the compass.

Discuss how ships' navigators, aircraft pilots and explorers use bearings to show direction of travel. A bearing of an object or place is the angle measured clockwise from north to the object or place. It is measured in degrees and always has three digits so, for example, 5° is given as 005°. Bearings can be measured with an ordinary circular protractor provided the angles less than 100° are written as three-digit numbers.

Give the children practice in estimating and measuring bearings. For example, what is the bearing of the bicycle from A?

Ask the children to draw a map of an island and mark on it the treasure, a wreck, and two other features. Show north and ask the children to find the bearing from each of the three places to the treasure.

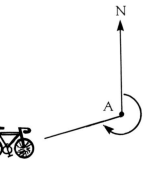

LINKS WITH THE ENVIRONMENT   Talk about the use of angles, bearings and parallel lines in everyday life.

- Parallel lines in the environment – such as railway lines, telegraph poles, window frames
- Intersecting lines on board games, interwoven fences, maps, tartans and ginghams, weaving
- Angles in constructions such as pylons, railway structures, houses, construction kits
- Congruent shapes in patterns and designs
- Navigation methods – using compasses and bearings

NOTES ON INVESTIGATIONS

Section A

A concave quadrilateral with one reflex and three acute angles may be drawn.

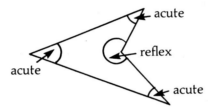

However, a quadrilateral with four acute angles cannot be drawn, as its interior angles would not add up to 360°. Do the children try other combinations of angles? For example:

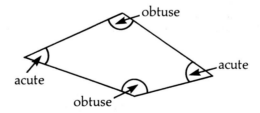

Section B

Do the children arrange four lines in various positions to make sets of equal angles?

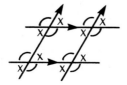

The maximum number of equal angles is 16, in this arrangement:

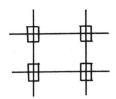

Section C

Check that the children measure the bearings correctly. They should discover that there is a difference of 180° between the bearings.

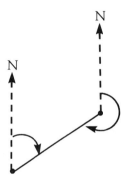

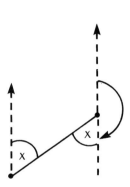

Measurement 1

Purpose

- To revise the notion of scale in simple drawings
- To introduce the use of unitary ratios
- To introduce height-finding techniques

Materials

Squared paper, rulers, plain paper, clinometer, long tape measure, reference books about sport and famous buildings

Vocabulary

Scale, measurements, scale drawing, represent, angle, clinometer, angle of elevation, horizontal, vertical, estimate

TEACHING POINTS   SECTION A

1 Revising scale

Remind the children that scale drawings are drawn smaller than life size for convenience of handling and measuring.

Revise the 1 cm: 1 m and 1 cm: 2 m scales (see pupils' book 1, 'Length') and discuss when it might be appropriate to use them – for example, when drawing a scale plan of the classroom, school hall or a sports pitch.

2 Investigating other scales

Explain that we can use whatever scale we find convenient.

Discuss the scale appropriate to use when drawing graphs or diagrams to show the heights of children in the class. For example, we might use a 1 cm: 10 cm scale where 1 cm represents 10 cm. Let the children draw the following people on squared paper, using a 1 cm: 10 cm scale.

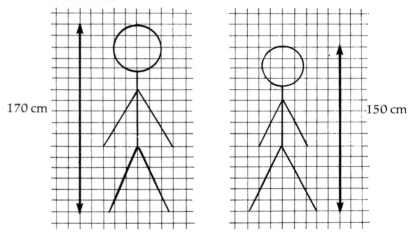

Ask them to draw some more people to the same scale and to state how tall they are on the drawing and in real life.

3 Comparing scales

Ask the children to compare scales. For example, let them draw on squared paper a tree that is 80 m tall, using a 1 cm: 10 m scale and a 1 cm: 20 m scale. What do they notice about the two drawings?

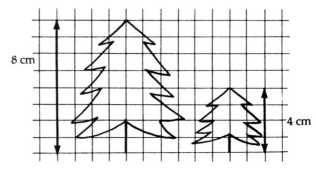

As the scale doubles, the height of the drawing halves.

SECTIONS B AND C

4 Using the unitary ratio 1:100

Explain that a scale of '1 cm represents 1 metre' is the same as '1 cm represents 100 cm'. This can be written as the unitary ratio 1:100. Discuss what 2 cm would represent (200 cm or 2 metres).

A game to play

SCALE IT UP

Prepare some cards showing lengths in centimetres, $\boxed{2\,\text{cm}}$, $\boxed{8\,\text{cm}}$, $\boxed{5\,\text{cm}}$, $\boxed{24\,\text{cm}}$, $\boxed{18\,\text{cm}}$, etc. and one card showing the unitary ratio: $\boxed{1:100}$.

  Prop the unitary ratio card on the table facing the children. Shuffle the other cards and then hold them up one at a time. The children have to state what the lengths shown would be in reality. The answers may be written down or given following the raising of a hand. They may be given in cm or metres.

5 Other unitary ratios

Talk about other unitary ratios. For example, if the ratio is 1:50, what would 1 cm represent? (50 cm or $\frac{1}{2}$ metre). If the ratio is 1:10, what does 1 cm represent? (10 cm or $\frac{1}{10}$ metre).

A game to play

SCALES

This is an extension of the game played in activity 4. Use the cards showing lengths in centimetres as before but extend the ratio cards to include other unitary ratios. For example: $\boxed{1:100}$, $\boxed{1:50}$, $\boxed{1:10}$, $\boxed{1:5}$.

  Shuffle both sets of cards and place them face downwards on a table. Pick up one from each pile. For example:

$$\boxed{1:50} \qquad \boxed{4\,\text{cm}}$$

The children have to state what the lengths shown would be in reality, using the ratios shown. Answers may be given in cm or metres.

6 Using scale to find heights

Discuss with the children how to find heights using a scale drawing method and a clinometer.

(a)   Walk a convenient distance away from a building. For example 30 m
(b)   Find the angle of elevation, using a clinometer.
(c)   Draw a scale drawing of the distances on squared paper, using a convenient scale such as 1:500 (or 1 cm:5 m).

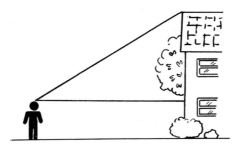

(d)   Find the height (not forgetting to add on the viewer's eye level).

This method is used as an activity in section C but you may wish to attempt it as a class activity.

Where appropriate, you might like to use the method of finding a position where the angle of elevation is 45° (a set square may be used). This means that the height of the object (from eye level) is the same as the distance away:

distance = height
total height = distance + eye level height

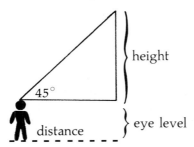

MENTAL WORK   The games suggested in activities 4 and 5 are appropriate mental work. In addition, the following may be attempted:

- Ask such questions as: the scale on a drawing is '1 cm represents 2 m'. What is the ratio? (1:200)
- Ask them to convert lengths in centimetres to metres. For example, 600 cm = ☐ m.

USING THE CALCULATOR   Use the calculator to work out unitary ratios. For example, if 3 cm represents 15 m, what is the ratio?

LINKS WITH THE ENVIRONMENT   Talk with the children about situations in everyday life which involve using scale and height finding.

- Looking at scales on maps and drawings
- Looking at plans of buildings
- Using scale in model making
- Talking about people who use clinometers, for example architects and surveyors

NOTES ON INVESTIGATIONS

Section A

Do the children use reference material to find the dimensions of a sports pitch, or do they find the measurements practically? Do they devise an appropriate scale that allows the drawing to fit on their page whilst covering most of the page?

Section B

Do the children calculate the real area of the flag to be $110 \text{ cm} \times 80 \text{ cm} = 8800 \text{ cm}^2$ and the area of the $1:10$ scale drawing to be $11 \text{ cm} \times 8 \text{ cm} = 88 \text{ cm}^2$? Do they realise that the $1:10$ scale gives an area of $\frac{1}{100} = \left(\frac{1}{10}\right)^2$ of the real area of the flag? Do they try this for other rectangles and find that this always happens with a $1:10$ scale?

Do they calculate the area of $1:5$ scale drawing to be $22 \text{ cm} \times 16 \text{ cm} = 352 \text{ cm}^2$? Do they realise that this is $\frac{1}{25}$ of the real area of the flag and that the $1:5$ scale gives an area of $\frac{1}{25} = \left(\frac{1}{5}\right)^2$ of the real area of the flag?

Section C

Do the children use reference material to find the heights of some famous buildings? Do they make a rational estimation of what the height of a single 'floor' might be and then estimate the approximate number of floors? Do they use a calculator to find out how many times taller the building is than them?

Number 4

Purpose

- To revise fractions and decimal notation in the context of measurement
- To introduce decimals and decimal places

Materials

Ruler, card, scissors, glue, paper, squared paper, blank hundred square, calculator

Vocabulary

Centimetre, millimetre (mm), perimeter, rectangle, approximately, rounded, fraction, decimal fraction, decimals, tenths, hundredths, decimal point, half

TEACHING POINTS   **SECTION A**

1 Measuring in centimetres and tenths of centimetres

Discuss how to measure an object which is not an exact number of centimetres in length. We need a ruler marked in tenths of a centimetre (i.e. millimetres). Each centimetre is divided into 10 equal parts, so each part is $\frac{1}{10}$ cm.

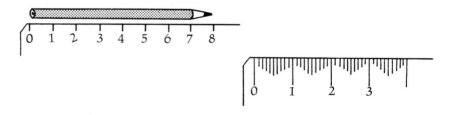

2 Say it another way

Discuss how we say or write centimetres and millimetres. For example, 3 cm 2 mm is $3\frac{2}{10}$ cm. This can be written as

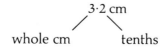

and is read as 'three point two centimetres'.

A game to play

ANOTHER WAY?

Make a number of flash cards showing various lengths in cm and mm. For example, $\boxed{3 \cdot 2 \text{ cm}}$, $\boxed{4\frac{3}{10} \text{ cm}}$, $\boxed{5 \text{ cm } 6 \text{ mm}}$. Shuffle the cards and place them face downwards. Hold them up one at a time for the children to see. The children then have to write two alternative ways of writing the lengths.

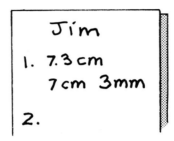

3 'Nought point . . .'

Discuss what happens when an object measures less than a whole centimetre, for example, 7 mm. We write, or say, 'nought point seven centimetres'

$$0 \cdot 7 \text{ cm}$$

no whole   just 7 mm
cm   or 7 tenths of a cm

4 Measuring lines

Give the children some lines to draw with a ruler and ask them to write the results in a chart. The lines must use cm and mm. Point out that 14·6 cm is

1 ten + 4 units + 6 tenths = $10 + 4 + \frac{6}{10}$.

For example:

tens	units	·	tenths
	3	·	4
1	4	·	6

SECTIONS B AND C

5 Writing decimals

Use squared paper to show a whole strip of ten squares and colour three of the squares. Ask the children what fraction is coloured ($\frac{3}{10}$).

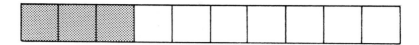

Discuss how this may be written in decimal form:

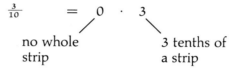

$\frac{3}{10}$ = 0 . 3

no whole strip   3 tenths of a strip

Look at other numbers, for example, $\frac{5}{10} = 0.5$, $\frac{9}{10} = 0.9$, etc. Put out some coloured strips to join the above strip.

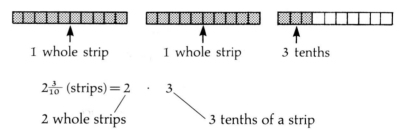

1 whole strip   1 whole strip   3 tenths

$2\frac{3}{10}$ (strips) = 2 . 3

2 whole strips   3 tenths of a strip

Show decimals as a decimal abacus. (An ordinary abacus can be converted into a decimal one for this purpose.)

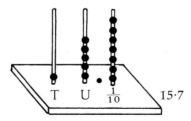

T   U $\frac{1}{10}$ 15·7

This is another way to show decimals:

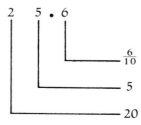

2   5 . 6

$\frac{6}{10}$

5

20

Give the children practice in this.

Ask the children to draw strips on squared paper to show given decimals, for example, 1·4.

A game to play

PUT THEM IN ORDER

Make a set of decimal cards. For example, | 5·2 |, | 0·9 |, | 7·7 | etc.
Shuffle the pack and hold up two cards. The children have to write the two decimals, smallest (or largest) first.

6 Looking at hundredths

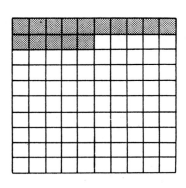

Use a blank hundred square and colour 15 squares. Discuss how this is $\frac{15}{100}$ of the square, or $\frac{1}{10} + \frac{5}{100}$.

Explain that we can write $\frac{15}{100}$ as a decimal:

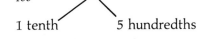

$$\frac{15}{100} = \qquad 0·15$$

1 tenth   5 hundredths

Give the children practice in writing fractions as decimals (e.g. $\frac{27}{100} \rightarrow 0·27$) and vice versa (e.g. $0·59 \rightarrow \frac{59}{100}$).

7 Decimal places

Talk to the children about decimal places. For example, 0·2 is written to 1 decimal place (after the point), and 0·23 is written to 2 decimal places (after the point).

8 Changing other fractions to decimals

Ask the children to change $\frac{1}{2}$ to hundredths, and to write the answer as a decimal:

$$\frac{1}{2} = \frac{50}{100} = 0·50 \text{ or } 0·5$$

Ask them to divide 1 by 2 on their calculator and 50 by 100. What do they find?
Explain that the calculator may be used to convert fractions to decimals.
Ask the children to change $\frac{3}{4}$ to hundredths and a decimal.

$$\frac{3}{4} = \frac{75}{100} = 0·75$$

Ask them to divide 3 by 4 and 75 by 100 on their calculator. What do they notice?

9 Horizontal to vertical recording

Write an addition of two numbers horizontally, for example,
$2 \cdot 5 + 16 \cdot 4$. Ask the children to record this vertically, lining up the
decimal points:

$$
\begin{array}{r}
2 \cdot 5 \\
+\, 16 \cdot 4 \\
\hline
\end{array}
$$

Point out that the addition process is as for HTU.

MENTAL WORK   Give the children practice in converting fractions to decimals and
vice versa, for example:

$$\frac{3}{10} = 0 \cdot 3, \qquad \frac{76}{100} = 0 \cdot 76, \qquad 0 \cdot 4 = \frac{4}{10}, \qquad 0 \cdot 27 = \frac{27}{100}$$

Give them practice in writing halves and quarters as decimals.

USING THE CALCULATOR   Let the children compare fractions by converting them to decimals
and writing them in order. For example, $\frac{4}{5}$ $(\frac{8}{10})$ and $\frac{9}{12}$ $(\frac{3}{4})$.

$$0 \cdot 80 > 0 \cdot 75$$

Give them practice in checking the results of simple addition of
decimals, for example, $1 \cdot 22 + 3 \cdot 79$.

$$
\begin{array}{r}
1 \cdot 22 \\
+\, 3 \cdot 79 \\
\hline
5 \cdot 01 \\
\hline
\end{array}
$$

LINKS WITH THE ENVIRONMENT   Talk about everyday situations which involve decimals.

- Currency, for example, $2·98, £1·37
- Measures, for example, 2·09 cm
- Timing in sporting activities such as athletics, swimming,
  skiing, car rallies – 10·8 seconds.

NOTES ON INVESTIGATIONS   **Section A**

Do the children design a suitable pop-up card? Do they measure
carefully and show their measurements in cm and mm, using correct
notation?

Section B

Do the children convert the fractions to decimals?

$$\frac{3}{4} \rightarrow 0.75 \quad \text{and} \quad \frac{4}{5} \rightarrow \frac{8}{10} \rightarrow 0.80$$

Do they appreciate that 0·76, 0·77, 0·78, 0·79 can all fit between the two fractions? Are they able to write the decimals as fractions?

$$\frac{76}{100}, \quad \frac{77}{100}, \quad \frac{78}{100}, \quad \frac{79}{100}$$

Extension work might involve a consideration of thousandths.

Section C

Do the children devise a logical approach to the investigation? For example:

$$\frac{1}{2} \rightarrow \frac{50}{100} \rightarrow \frac{49}{100} \rightarrow 0.49$$

$$\frac{1}{2} \rightarrow \frac{500}{1000} \rightarrow \frac{499}{1000} \rightarrow 0.499$$

$$\frac{1}{2} \rightarrow \frac{5000}{10\,000} \rightarrow \frac{4999}{10\,000} \rightarrow 0.4999$$

and so on. Do the children realise that this could go on indefinitely?

Co-ordinates

Purpose

- To revise co-ordinates in the first quadrant
- To introduce co-ordinates in all four quadrants

Materials

Squared paper, extra paper for written work and drawings

Vocabulary

Grid, co-ordinates, horizontal axis, vertical axis, vertices, shortest route, longest route, distance, instructions, quadrant, positions, change of direction, line of symmetry, straight lines, dice

TEACHING POINTS   SECTION A

1 Revision of vocabulary

Remind the children that co-ordinates are a pair of numbers which fix a point on a graph or grid. Remind them that the main horizontal and vertical lines on the graph or grid are called axes. Can they tell you which is the vertical axis and which is the horizontal? Reference to the horizon may give them a clue.

2 Plotting co-ordinates

Draw a grid on the board to remind the children how both axes are numbered, and that the point where the axes meet is numbered (0, 0). Remind them how co-ordinates are written, i.e. (2, 3). These are ordered pairs of numbers so the order of the numbers is important. Do they remember to write the horizontal number first and then the vertical one? Can they plot the point (2, 3) on the grid? Give the children practice in plotting other co-ordinates.

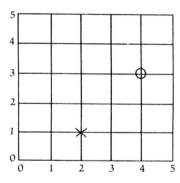

A game to play

FOUR IN LINE

This game can be played in pairs. Each pair draws a 5 × 5 grid or uses a duplicated grid.

The first player in the pair calls out the co-ordinates for a position on the grid which they then mark with a cross, e.g. (2, 1). The second player calls out the co-ordinates for another position on the grid and they mark that with a circle or dot, e.g. (4, 3). The players continue to do this until one of them has made a line of four co-ordinate points – horizontally, vertically or diagonally. If a player calls out the co-ordinates and plots their position wrongly on the grid, they lose that turn.

As the children play, they should begin to be aware of the strategy involved in blocking their opponent's line of 4.

3 Plotting shapes

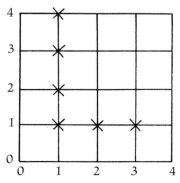

Give the children practice in plotting the vertices of letters, e.g. L, T, and the vertices of plane shapes. Ask them to join the vertices with straight lines, and to write the co-ordinates for their shapes.

A game to play

CODES

This game is for two or more teams or groups.
Draw a grid on the board. Give each co-ordinate point the name of a letter. For example:

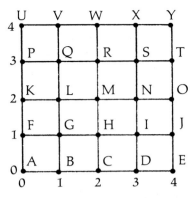

Write on the board the co-ordinates for a word, for example (2, 2), (0, 0), (4, 3), (2, 1), (3, 3). The first team or group to find the word scores a point.

SECTIONS B AND C

4 Four quadrants

Show the children, by drawing a grid on the board or a large piece of squared paper, how the two axes can be extended to show four quadrants. Explain that the point where the axes cross is numbered 0 and represents zero on both axes. Can the children suggest what the numbering will be on the extended axes? Do they appreciate that these will be negative numbers?

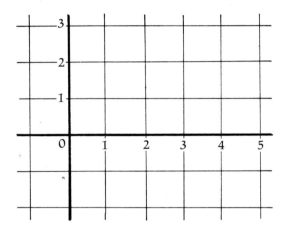

Give the children practice in drawing and numbering a grid with all four quadrants. Talk about how the quadrants are called first, second, third and fourth, depending on their position. The first one has only positive co-ordinates. The other quadrants are counted anti-clockwise from this one.

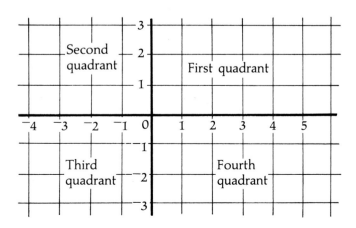

5 Plotting co-ordinates

Point out to the children that when plotting co-ordinate positions on a grid with four quadrants they still plot the position of the first number of the pair along the horizontal axis, and the position of the second number along the vertical one. Use a grid, drawn on the board or on a large piece of 2 cm squared paper, to give the children practice in plotting co-ordinates in all four quadrants.

6 Draw grids and plotting positions

Let the children work in pairs. Ask them to draw a grid with four quadrants. The grid can be a map of an imaginary place and they can mark on it four or more of its features, e.g. a haunted castle. There must be at least one feature in each quadrant. They must then list each place on a separate piece of paper and write its co-ordinates.

    They can then exchange grids with another pair of children and check the accuracy of each other's co-ordinates.

A game to play

FIND THE CO-ORDINATES

This game is for two players and a referee.

    Each player has their own grid. They keep this grid hidden from their opponent. They mark eight positions on it with a cross, two positions in each quadrant. They take it in turns to call out a pair of co-ordinates. If they score a hit, i.e. they give the co-ordinates for the position of one of their opponent's positions, their opponent rings that cross. The first player to score four hits on their opponent's grid wins the game.

    The referee can check the accuracy of the co-ordinates.

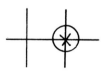

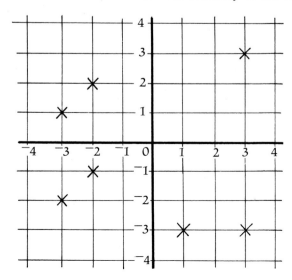

7 Symmetrical shapes

Draw a grid on the board and ask the children to copy it. Give them the co-ordinates for points in the first quadrant which, when joined by straight lines, will make a simple shape.

Ask them to give the co-ordinates for a shape symmetrical to it in the second quadrant, or the fourth quadrant. This activity can be developed and extended according to the understanding and capability of the children.

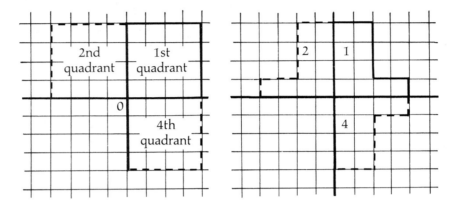

8 Patterns

Use a grid with all four quadrants marked.
Ask the children to make a pattern by joining up the co-ordinates.
For example:

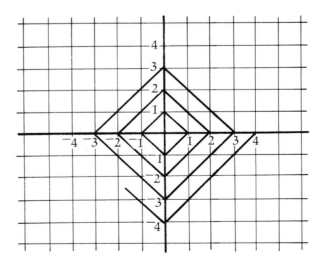

Can the children state the co-ordinates that have been joined? Can they recognise the shapes made?

Some patterns are often seen in a curved drawing or stitching designs.

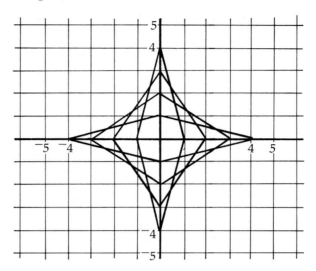

A game to play

FOLLOW THE LEADER

Give each child in a group a grid with all four quadrants marked.

One of the group plots and joins the co-ordinates for a route on their grid, using all four quadrants. They do not show this to the other members of the groups but call out the co-ordinates for the route, in order of travel. The other children plot and join these co-ordinates on their grids. They don't let anyone else see their grids until everyone has finished. Then they compare their routes with the original one to see whose is identical with it.

LINKS WITH THE ENVIRONMENT   Talk with the children about using co-ordinates in everyday life.

- Finding places on maps and plans
- Looking for co-ordinates on Ordnance Survey maps
- Playing computer co-ordinate games
- Playing board games, for example Battleships
- Curve stitching

NOTES ON INVESTIGATIONS

Section A

Do the children realise that the order of the co-ordinate numbers is important and that when the numbers are reversed, it usually indicates a different point? Do the children make a list of the co-ordinates of the planets and check carefully for pairs of numbers that are reversed?

Section B

Do the children read and conform to the rules of travel? Do they find these different routes and state the co-ordinates for each change of direction? Do they find the shortest route to be 14 units?

Section C

Do the children design a game that involves using all four quadrants? Do they devise logical rules?

Purpose

- To revise line graphs
- To understand conversion graphs
- To interpret information through two-way tables
- To interpret network diagrams

Materials

Squared paper, leaflets or newspapers showing exchange rates for different currencies, atlas or geography reference books for Europe

Vocabulary

Miles, steady, speed, distance travelled, time, line graph, approximately, French francs, German marks, pound, amount, exchange rate, round, nearest whole number, table, route, Europe, steeper, units of foreign currency, appropriate two-way table

TEACHING POINTS   **SECTION A**

1 Line graphs

Revise the drawing and interpretation of line graphs. Ask the children to draw a line graph from data in a table. For example:

Time	9 a.m.	10 a.m.	11 a.m.	12 noon	1 p.m.	2 p.m.	3 p.m.
Temperature	2 °C	3 °C	5 °C	7 °C	7 °C	6 °C	5 °C

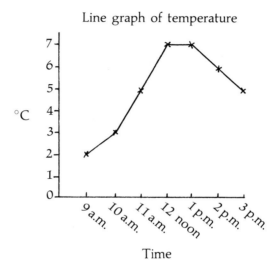

Line graph of temperature

Remind them again to number the axes correctly and put both labels on the axes and a title. Ask the children to interpret the graph by answering questions or by writing sentences about it.

2 Constant speed

Talk about vehicles travelling at a constant speed – for example, cars on a motorway, express trains or aeroplanes.

Ask the children to complete a table for a car journey travelling at 50 miles an hour on a motorway (miles or kilometres can be used at the teacher's discretion). Point out that at the start of the journey the distance travelled is 0 miles and the time taken is 0 hours.

Hours	0	1	2	3	4	5	6	7
Miles	0	50	100					

Draw and label the axes for the graph. Can the children suggest an appropriate scale for the distance axis? One scale might use 50 mile intervals. See if the children can predict what the graph will be like by looking at the completed table (a straight line). Ask them to plot the co-ordinates for the graph and complete it.

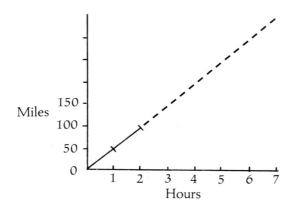

Check they can interpret the graph by asking questions.

How far will the car have travelled after $1\frac{1}{2}$ hours?
How long did it take the car to travel 225 miles?

A game to play

STEADY SPEED

The game can be played by two players or teams.
Draw a table:

Hours	1	2	3	4	5	6
Distance in km						

The first player writes a distance in the first of the empty distance boxes, for example , 7 km.

Hours	1	2	3	4	5	6
Distance in km	7					

The other player has to complete the other five distance boxes correctly, assuming a steady or constant speed. A calculator may be used to check that the distances travelled are increasing at a steady rate. One point is scored for each correctly completed table. The players then change over. The first player to score 7 points is the winner.

An alternative game is to time the players completing the distance table with a stop watch. The quickest scores 1 point.

3 Stopping

Talk about situations where the driver of the car may stop for an hour's rest. What happens to the table and the graph?

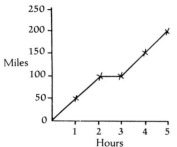

Hours	0	1	2	3	4	5
Miles	0	50	100	100	150	200

4 Intersecting graphs

Draw a table to show how two girls walked at a steady speed for 6 km with a 15 minutes' rest.

Ann and Barbara's journey:

Time	9:00	9:15	9:30	9:45	10:00	10:15	10:30	10:45
Distance in km	0	1	2	3	4	4	5	6

Ask the children to draw the graph of the girls' journey. For example:

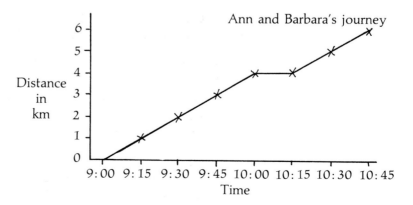

Robert and Tom set off at 9:30a.m. and cycled the 6 km at a constant speed and arrived at 10 o'clock. Ask the children to show the boys' journey on the same graph.

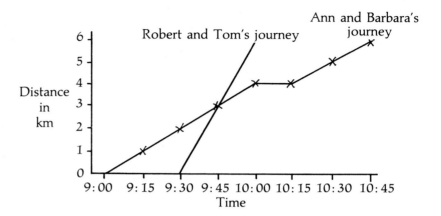

Ask the children questions about the graph.

> How long did it take the girls to travel the 6 km?
> At what time did the boys pass the girls?
> How far had the girls travelled when the boys passed them?
> How many km per hour were the girls walking?
> At what time would the boys have had to set off if they were to arrive at the same time as the girls? What would this graph look like?

5 Comparing speeds

Talk with the children about travelling the same distance but by different types of transport. For example, travelling across the Atlantic Ocean from Britain to America by Concorde, ocean liner or hot-air balloon. Ask which would be the quickest and which the slowest.

Draw one graph to show all the different ways of travelling. Can the children explain why some of the line graphs are steeper than others?

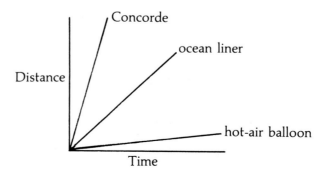

SECTION B

6 Conversion tables

Talk about how conversion tables are often used by travel agents and banks to convert currency, for example, from pounds to dollars. Draw a partly completed table showing conversions of £ and $. Ask the children to complete it, assuming that £1 is worth $2 (this varies, of course).

£	1	2	3	4	5	6	7	8	9	10
$	2	4	6							

The game 'Steady speed' (activity 2) could be played using £ and other currencies instead of hours and distance respectively.

7 Conversion graphs

Talk about how straight line graphs can be used as conversion graphs. Ask the children to complete the straight line graph using the table converting £ to $.

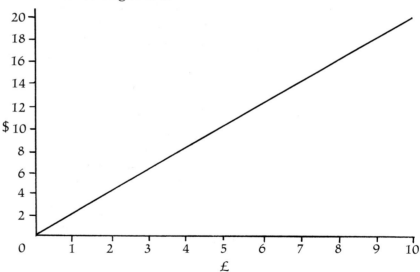

Ask the children questions about the graph.

> How many dollars is £6 worth?
> How many pounds is $18 worth?
> How many dollars could I exchange for £10?

The children are asked to use a conversion graph to work out exchange rates for the pound in other currencies in the pupils' book.

Conversion graphs for petrol (litres/gallons), distance–time graphs and temperature (Fahrenheit to Celsius) could also be discussed.

SECTION C

8 Two-way table

Talk with the children about constructing, describing and interpreting information through two-way tables. Draw a simple two-way table to record the orders taken from four people in a café.

	Soup	Chips	Fish	Peas	Pie
Mary	✓	✓	✓	✓	
Andrew		✓		✓	✓
Tom	✓		✓		
Jean				✓	✓

Ask the children questions about the orders.

What did Andrew order?
How many people ordered peas?
How many people ordered pie and chips? Who were they?

Ask a group of children to make a two-way table to show what food they would like to order from a café or restaurant. Can other children interpret it?

9 Distance charts

Draw a simple distance chart of several towns or cities.

Aberdeen				
420	Birmingham			
493	81	Bristol		
458	100	144	Cambridge	
576	176	186	125	Dover

Distance in miles

Ask the children to answer questions using the distance chart.

How far is it from Birmingham to Cambridge?
How much further is it from Dover to Bristol than from Dover to Birmingham?

A more complex distance chart could be used showing distances in miles and kilometres. For example,

Aberdeen				
420 (676 km)	Birmingham			
493 (793 km)	81 (130 km)	Bristol		
458 (737 km)	100 (161 km)	144 (232 km)	Cambridge	
576 (927 km)	176 (283 km)	186 (299 km)	125 (201 km)	Dover

Distance in miles and kilometres

Distance in miles can be converted into kilometres (approximately) by multiplying by 1·6.

10 Networks

Draw a network diagram of the local area or of local towns. Write on the distances. Discuss how to find the shortest route between places, for example, from Dover to Sevenoaks.

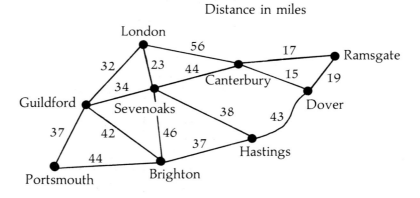

Distance in miles

MENTAL WORK Ask the children questions involving conversions. For example, if £1 is worth $2, how many dollars are £27 worth?

USING THE CALCULATOR Ask the children to look in newspapers and find the exact exchange rates for different currencies. Ask them to use their calculator to convert £10, £15, etc. into other currencies.

LINKS WITH THE ENVIRONMENT

- Talk about everyday situations involving line and conversion graphs and collect data from newspapers and magazines showing these. For example, look at conversion graphs and tables for money (rates of exchange), petrol (litres/gallons).
- Look in holiday brochures and road atlases for two-way tables and distance charts.
- Look for network diagrams in everyday life – roads, train routes, tram routes, air routes, etc.

NOTES ON INVESTIGATIONS

Section A

Do the children choose sensible ways to travel from home to school (for example, walk, by car, by bus, cycle)? Are their estimates of the time taken for each reasonable? Do they choose a sensible type of graph to record the data?

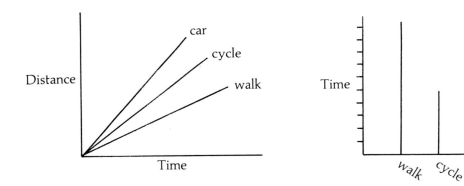

Does the graph they draw show all three ways of travelling from home to school? Do they label the axes correctly?

Section B

(It would be useful to have leaflets, newspapers or books showing the exchange rates for different countries.)
Do the children round the exchange rates accurately (when appropriate) to the nearest whole number? Are the children's questions about exchange rates appropriate for others to answer?

Section C

(It would be useful to have an atlas or reference books showing the capital cities in Europe.) Do they record their data in a two-way table?
Do their written explanations show that they can interpret two-way tables correctly?

Number 5

Purpose

- To revise fractions of quantities, and equivalences
- To revise addition of fractions with the same denominator
- To introduce subtraction of fractions with the same denominator
- To introduce addition of fractions with different denominators
- To use simple percentages
- To calculate fractions and percentages of quantities, using a calculator where necessary
- To convert fractions to percentages

Materials

Calculators, squared paper

Vocabulary

Percentage, fraction, fraction chart, divided exactly, table, share, amounts, cost, sale items, cheapest, most expensive, marked price, discount

TEACHING POINTS   **SECTION A**

1 Half, quarter, eighth of quantities

Remind the children about finding fractions of quantities and how this is recorded. Put 16 counters on a table. Ask a child to divide or share them into half. Talk about methods of recording this. For example:

$$\text{OOOOOOOO/OOOOOOOO}$$
$$\tfrac{1}{2} \text{ of } 16 = 8$$
$$16 \div 2 = 8$$

Similarly ask children to divide the 16 counters into quarters and later eighths.

Can they find $\tfrac{3}{4}$ of 16 and $\tfrac{5}{8}$ of 16? Talk about methods for showing these. For example:

$$\text{OOOO/OOOO/OOOO/OOOO}$$
$$\tfrac{1}{4} \text{ of } 16 = 4$$
$$\tfrac{3}{4} \text{ of } 16 = 12$$

2 Other fractions of quantities

Use similar activities to find algorithms for other fraction families, for example $\frac{1}{3}$, $\frac{1}{6}$ and $\frac{1}{5}$, $\frac{1}{10}$. Ask the children to show the fraction of quantities both as a diagram and as a fraction sentence.

3 Colouring fractions

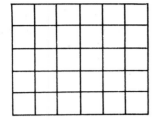

Give the children practice in colouring fractions of shapes on squared paper. For example, draw a shape using 30 squares and ask them to colour $\frac{1}{3}$ red, $\frac{2}{5}$ blue, $\frac{1}{10}$ green, $\frac{1}{6}$ yellow.

4 Fractions of quantities

Can the children calculate fractions of quantities?

$\frac{1}{3}$ of 30   (10)
$\frac{2}{5}$ of 30   (12)
$\frac{1}{10}$ of 30   (3)
$\frac{1}{6}$ of 30   (5)

Ask them to calculate fractions of other numbers and quantities.

5 Simple equivalence

Draw fraction walls and remind the children how to use them to find equivalence.

1	
$\frac{1}{2}$	$\frac{1}{2}$
$\frac{1}{4}$ $\frac{1}{4}$ $\frac{1}{4}$ $\frac{1}{4}$	
$\frac{1}{8}$ $\frac{1}{8}$ $\frac{1}{8}$ $\frac{1}{8}$ $\frac{1}{8}$ $\frac{1}{8}$ $\frac{1}{8}$ $\frac{1}{8}$	

1
$\frac{1}{3}$ $\frac{1}{3}$ $\frac{1}{3}$
$\frac{1}{6}$ $\frac{1}{6}$ $\frac{1}{6}$ $\frac{1}{6}$ $\frac{1}{6}$ $\frac{1}{6}$

1
$\frac{1}{5}$ $\frac{1}{5}$ $\frac{1}{5}$ $\frac{1}{5}$ $\frac{1}{5}$
$\frac{1}{10}$ $\frac{1}{10}$ $\frac{1}{10}$ $\frac{1}{10}$ $\frac{1}{10}$ $\frac{1}{10}$ $\frac{1}{10}$ $\frac{1}{10}$ $\frac{1}{10}$ $\frac{1}{10}$

Talk about the number patterns.

$$1 = \frac{2}{2} = \frac{3}{3} = \frac{4}{4} = \frac{5}{5} = \frac{6}{6} = \frac{8}{8} = \frac{10}{10}$$

How could 1 be shown in sevenths or ninths?

Similarly, talk about other equivalence fraction patterns. Can they explain them?

$$\frac{1}{2} = \frac{2}{4} = \frac{3}{6} = \frac{4}{8} = \frac{5}{10}$$
$$\frac{1}{4} = \frac{2}{8} \qquad \frac{3}{4} = \frac{6}{8}$$
$$\frac{1}{3} = \frac{2}{6} \qquad \frac{2}{3} = \frac{4}{6}$$
$$\frac{1}{5} = \frac{2}{10} \qquad \frac{2}{5} = \frac{4}{10} \qquad \frac{3}{5} = \frac{6}{10} \qquad \frac{4}{5} = \frac{8}{10} \text{ etc.}$$

Games to play

EQUIVALENT FRACTIONS

Play the game in two teams.

A child from the first team writes a fraction (for example, $\frac{2}{3}$) and a player from the other team has to write two equivalent fractions (for example, $\frac{4}{6}, \frac{8}{12}$). They score a point for each correct fraction. The teams change over. The initial fraction ($\frac{2}{3}$ in this case) cannot be used to start again. The first team to score 20 points wins.

EQUIVALENCE SNAP

This is a game for two players.

Make a set of equivalent fraction cards:

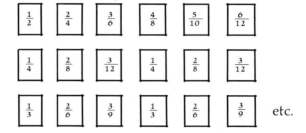

Shuffle and deal the cards equally between the players, who stack their cards face down in front of them. The dealer turns over her top card and places it face up in the centre of the table. The second player turns over her top card. If the two cards are equivalent fractions, the first player to call 'Snap' wins the cards, places them at the bottom of her pile and restarts the game. If the fractions are not equivalent, the turn passes to the dealer. The game ends when one player has won all the cards.

6 Numerator and denominator

Introduce or revise the words 'numerator' and 'denominator'. Explain their meanings.

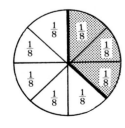

$$\frac{\text{number of shaded parts}}{\text{total number of parts}} = \frac{3}{8}$$

Write some fractions for example, $\frac{5}{8}, \frac{9}{10}$. Ask the children which number in each fraction is the numerator and which the denominator.

7 Adding fractions with the same denominator

Let the children draw shapes on squared paper to show the addition of fractions. Talk about the recording. For example:

$$\tfrac{1}{4}+\tfrac{1}{4}=\tfrac{2}{4}$$

$$\tfrac{3}{10}+\tfrac{4}{10}=\tfrac{7}{10}$$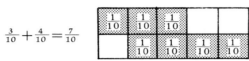

Write a fraction on the board such as $\tfrac{5}{6}$ and ask a child to write a fraction sentence for it, for example,

$$\tfrac{1}{6}+\tfrac{4}{6}=\tfrac{5}{6}$$

Can anyone think of a different fraction sentence for $\tfrac{5}{6}$?

8 Subtraction of fractions

Talk about subtracting fractions using pictures or squared paper to provide imagery. For example:

$$\tfrac{5}{6}-\tfrac{1}{6}=\tfrac{4}{6}$$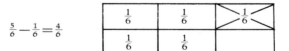

$$\tfrac{7}{8}-\tfrac{4}{8}=\tfrac{3}{8}$$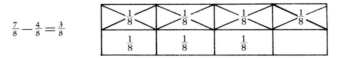

(Fraction walls are used in the pupils' book.)
Write a fraction on the board such as $\tfrac{3}{8}$ and ask a child to write a subtraction sentence for it, for example,

$$\tfrac{7}{8}-\tfrac{4}{8}=\tfrac{3}{8}$$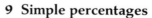

9 Simple percentages

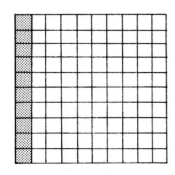

Ask the children to use squared paper to draw a 10 × 10 square. Ask them to colour 10 squares. What fraction of the 100 square have they coloured? ($\tfrac{10}{100}$ or $\tfrac{1}{10}$). Remind them that a short way of writing 'out of 100' is 'per cent' or %, i.e. $\tfrac{10}{100}=10\%$.
   Ask them to colour and record other fractions on the hundred square and show it both as a fraction of 100 and as a percentage.

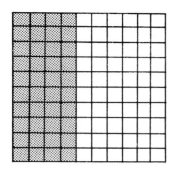

40 squares

$\frac{40}{100} = 40\%$

Ask the children to write fractions of 100 as percentages and vice versa.

$\frac{35}{100} = 35\%$ $\frac{27}{100} = 27\%$

$62\% = \frac{62}{100}$ $97\% = \frac{97}{100}$

Explain that any amount out of 100 can be shown as a percentage. For example:

53 out of 100 people are women $\rightarrow \frac{53}{100} = 53\%$

25 out of 100 birds are blackbirds $\rightarrow \frac{25}{100} = 25\%$

A game to play

CHANGE

Play the game in pairs or two teams. A player from the first team writes a fraction out of 100 on the board, for example, $\frac{62}{100}$. A child from the second team has to change the fraction into a percentage. Each correct answer scores 1 point. The winner is the first to score 11 points. The game could be adapted to changing percentages into fractions out of 100.

SECTION B AND C

10 Addition of fractions

Talk about addition of fractions from the same fraction family, for example,

$\frac{1}{4} + \frac{1}{8}$

Use pictures or the fraction wall to provide the imagery. For example:

$\frac{1}{4}$	$\frac{1}{8}$		

Remind them also about equivalence, i.e. $\frac{1}{4} = \frac{2}{8}$.

1							
$\frac{1}{2}$				$\frac{1}{2}$			
$\frac{1}{4}$		$\frac{1}{4}$		$\frac{1}{4}$		$\frac{1}{4}$	
$\frac{1}{8}$							

Talk about the methods of recording addition. Here is one way.

$$\tfrac{1}{4} + \tfrac{1}{8} =$$

$$\tfrac{2}{8} + \tfrac{1}{8} = \tfrac{3}{8}$$

Give the children practice in this.

Develop the work to include addition of fractions from different families, for example, $\tfrac{1}{3} + \tfrac{1}{4}$. Again use the fraction walls or pictures to provide the imagery to help their understanding. Explain how to find a common denominator using the equivalence patterns. For example:

$$\tfrac{1}{3} = \tfrac{2}{6} = \tfrac{3}{9} = \ \tfrac{4}{12}$$

$$\tfrac{1}{4} = \tfrac{2}{8} = \ \ \tfrac{3}{12}$$

Talk about the methods of recording. Here are two ways:

$$\tfrac{1}{3} + \tfrac{1}{4} = \qquad\qquad \tfrac{1}{3} + \tfrac{1}{4} =$$

$$\tfrac{4}{12} + \tfrac{3}{12} = \tfrac{7}{12} \qquad\quad \tfrac{4+3}{12} = \tfrac{7}{12}$$

Give the children practice in this.

The work on addition of fractions in the pupils' book is kept fairly simple. Some teachers might wish to develop the work to include the addition of mixed numbers, for example $1\tfrac{3}{4} + 2\tfrac{1}{2}$, and addition using improper fractions. Talk about the methods of recording. For example:

$$1\tfrac{3}{4} + 2\tfrac{1}{2} = \qquad\qquad 1\tfrac{3}{4} + 2\tfrac{1}{2} =$$

$$3\tfrac{3}{4} + \tfrac{1}{2} = \qquad\qquad \tfrac{7}{4} + \tfrac{5}{2} =$$

$$3\tfrac{3}{4} + \tfrac{2}{4} = \qquad\qquad \tfrac{7}{4} + \tfrac{10}{4} =$$

$$3\tfrac{5}{4} = \qquad\qquad\qquad \tfrac{17}{4} =$$

$$4\tfrac{1}{4} \qquad\qquad\qquad\quad 4\tfrac{1}{4}$$

11 Pencil and paper methods

Ask children to work out $\tfrac{2}{3}$ of £15.

$$\tfrac{1}{3} \text{ of £15} \rightarrow \text{£5}$$

$$\tfrac{2}{3} \text{ of £15} \rightarrow \text{£10}$$

Show how this can be done on a calculator.

12 Sale prices and discount

Explain to the children that the selling price of goods, such as clothes, shoes, etc. is 100%. However, shops often have a sale when goods are sold at a reduced or sale price, for example, $\tfrac{1}{2}$ price, $\tfrac{1}{3}$ off. Sometimes sale goods are sold at a discount price, such as 10% off the selling price.

Give the children practice in working out sale prices after a percentage discount or fraction has been deducted from the marked price. For example, find the cost of the following items:

coat £53 10% off	shirt £12·99 $\frac{1}{3}$ off

Talk about the methods of calculating these. For example:

10% of £53 is £5·30 $100\% - 10\% = 90\%$

£53 − £5·30 = £47·70   90% of £53 = £47·70

A game to play

MATCH THE PRICE

Play the game in two groups.

  Give each group an identical chart showing the original price of sale items, the discount offered and a matching set of sale price cards. For example:

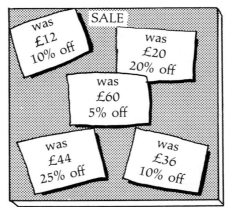

At a given signal the children use a calculator to work out the sale prices on the chart and match the sale price cards to the items. The first group to do it correctly wins.

  The game could be adapted to show holiday prices, the children calculating percentage reductions for children etc.

MENTAL WORK
- Revise finding $\frac{1}{2}, \frac{1}{4}, \frac{1}{5}, \frac{1}{10}$ of quantities such as 20.
- Revise finding $\frac{2}{3}, \frac{5}{8}, \frac{5}{6}$ of quantities such as 24.

- Write a fraction equal to $\frac{1}{3}, \frac{6}{8}$, etc.

- Write a fraction sentence for $\frac{7}{8}$.

- What is $\frac{7}{8} - \frac{2}{8}$?

- What is $\frac{75}{100}$ as a percentage?

- Ask verbal problems involving percentages. For example, 16 out of 100 people were boys. What percentage was this?

USING THE CALCULATOR Use the calculator to give the children practice in finding amounts. For example:

$\frac{1}{5}$ of £65 $\frac{3}{8}$ of £50 $\frac{4}{5}$ of 8 m

Check that the children can enter the problem accurately. For example:

$\frac{1}{5}$ of £65 → 1 $\boxed{\div}$ 5 $\boxed{\times}$ 65 $\boxed{=}$ or   65 $\boxed{\div}$ 5 $\boxed{=}$

Talk about the interpretation of the answer. For example,

$\frac{4}{5}$ of 8 m → 6·4 → 6 m 40 cm

Ask the children to calculate percentages of amounts of money, for example, 15% of £80. Explain that calculators vary in the key sequences required to work out the answer. One key sequence might be 80 $\boxed{\times}$ 15 $\boxed{\%}$ $\boxed{=}$.

Ask the children to change fractions to percentages. For example:

$\frac{1}{2} = \square\%$ $\frac{3}{8} = \square\%$

Remind them that when a fraction is changed into a percentage, it is first written as hundredths, for example, $\frac{1}{2} = \frac{50}{100}$. Can the children use their calculator to change a fraction into a percentage? One way might be

1 $\boxed{\div}$ 2 $\boxed{\%}$

What happens if we multiply the fraction by 100?

1 $\boxed{\div}$ 2 $\boxed{\times}$ 100 $\boxed{=}$

Talk about what happens if we try to change $\frac{1}{3}$, $\frac{1}{6}$, $\frac{1}{7}$ or $\frac{1}{9}$ into percentages.

Ask the children to use the calculator to change each fraction of an equivalent fraction pattern into a decimal and then a percentage. For example:

$\frac{3}{5} = \frac{6}{10} = \cdots$

$\frac{3}{5} = 0·6$ $\frac{6}{10} = 0·6$

$\frac{3}{5} = 60\%$ $\frac{6}{10} = 60\%$

so $\frac{3}{5} = \frac{6}{10} = 0·6 = 60\%$

A game to play

FIND THE NUMBER

Play the game in pairs or in two teams.
   The first child sets a problem for the second child. For example, find 10% of 200. A calculator is used to work out the answer. They then change over. Each correct answer scores 1 point. The first player to score 10 points is the winner.

LINKS WITH THE ENVIRONMENT   Talk about situations in everyday life involving fractions and percentages.

- Sharing activities – sharing pizzas, gateaux, sweets
- Art and craft – making patterns and designs using fractions, for example seed, lentil and pasta patterns stuck on card or paper pressed into Plasticine like a mosaic
- Sale items – fractions and percentages off the marked price
- Examinations – we talk about results as a percentage
- News programmes on radio and TV – for example, inflation at 10%
- Interest rates, mortgage rates, pay rises are usually stated in percentages.

NOTES ON INVESTIGATIONS

Section A

The number of cakes that divide exactly by $\frac{1}{2}$ or $\frac{1}{3}$ or $\frac{1}{4}$ must be multiples of 12; that is 12, 24, 36, 48, 60, 72, 84, 96. Similarly, in finding numbers of cakes less than 100 that divide exactly by $\frac{1}{2}$ or $\frac{1}{5}$ or $\frac{1}{10}$, the number must be a multiple of 10; that is, 10, 20, 30, 40, 50, 60, 70, 80, 90.

Section B

Do the children choose random amounts that total £100? Do they appreciate that the three amounts can be written as percentages of £100?

   £63 + £9 + £28 = £100
   63% + 9% + 28% = 100%

Do their explanations indicate that they understand the relationship between the amounts?

Section C

Do the children appreciate that 50% is $\frac{50}{100} = \frac{1}{2}$? The equivalent fractions for $\frac{1}{2}$ are:

$$\frac{1}{2} = \frac{2}{4} = \frac{3}{6} = \frac{4}{8} = \frac{5}{10} = \frac{6}{12} = \frac{7}{14} = \cdots = 50\%$$

The numerator is half the denominator each time.
   Similar relationships apply to 25% and 75%:

$$25\% = \frac{25}{100} = \frac{1}{4}$$

$$\frac{1}{4} = \frac{2}{8} = \frac{3}{12} = \frac{4}{16} = \frac{5}{20} = \frac{6}{24} = \cdots$$

$$75\% = \frac{75}{100} = \frac{3}{4}$$

$$\frac{3}{4} = \frac{6}{8} = \frac{9}{12} = \frac{12}{16} = \frac{15}{20} = \frac{18}{24} = \cdots$$

Number 6

Purpose

- To revise and use simple formulae
- To understand simple formulae and equations
- To express simple functions symbolically

Materials

Squared paper, calculator

Vocabulary

Rectangles, volume, perimeter, formula, pentagon, hexagon, octagon, triangle, square, area, pairs, length, width

TEACHING POINTS   SECTION A

1 How did we do it?

Revise the methods for finding the perimeter of a square, i.e. add the four sides together or measure one side and multiply by 4.
   Ask the children if they can explain how to find the area of a square.

2 Using rectangles

Ask the children if they can explain a method for finding the perimeter of a rectangle. For example:

- add all four sides together
- add any two adjacent sides and double the result
- double a short side, double a long side and add them

Ask them to explain different methods for finding the area of a rectangle, e.g. counting squares, area = length × width. Which is the most convenient to use?

3 More perimeters

Ask the children to use their methods for finding perimeters to find different rectangles with a perimeter of 20 cm. Discuss their methods when they have completed the task. For example, the long and shorter side must add up to 10 cm. This might be 9 cm + 1 cm, 8 cm + 2 cm, etc.

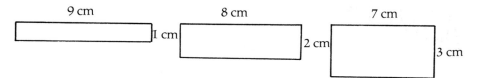

9 cm   1 cm   8 cm   2 cm   7 cm   3 cm

A game to play

FIND THE PERIMETER

Make a set of cards showing lengths marked in centimetres. For example, 3 cm , 7 cm , 5 cm etc. Shuffle the cards, place them face downwards on the table. Hold up two cards at a time and display them to the children, who have to state, or write, the perimeter of a rectangle with sides shown on the cards.

SECTIONS B AND C

4 Using symbols

Draw a road on the board or on paper.

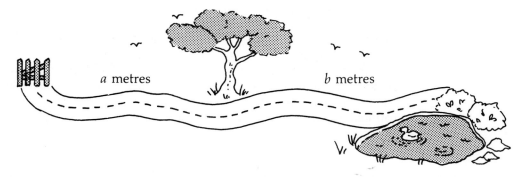

a metres   *b* metres

Explain that we don't know the distances from the gate to the tree and the tree to the pond so we use letters to stand for the distances.

Ask the children how we could work out the distance from the gate to the pond. (Add a metres and b metres.) Explain that this can be written as

distance to walk $= a$ metres $+ b$ metres
or $d = a + b$

(We say that d is the distance to be walked in metres, and a is the distance from the gate to the tree in metres and b is the distance from the tree to the pond in metres.) Explain that $d = a + b$ is the formula for finding the distance.

Ask the children to find the answer if the distance from the gate to the tree is 50 m and the distance from the tree to the pond is 100 m. Check that the children realise what is the value of a and b (50 and 100).

$$d = 50 + 100 = 150 \text{ (metres)}$$

Ask the children to find the value of d if $a = 40$ metres and $b = 80$ metres.

5 More paths

Draw another track or path system in the form of a quadrilateral.

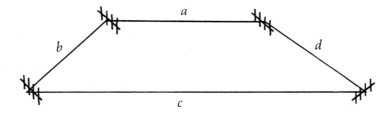

Ask the children to suggest letters to represent the four distances (for example, a, b, c, d) and a letter to represent the distance all the way round (e.g. p for 'perimeter'). Explain that we use different letters for different distances (hence d and p).

Ask them to devise a formula for the perimeter and to explain which each letter means. For example:

$$p = a + b + c + d$$

Suggest values for a, b, c and d and let the children find the value of p.

6 More shapes

Ask the children to draw shapes of their own with five sides, using squared paper, where two sides are the same length. Discuss what formula might be appropriate for the perimeter. For example:

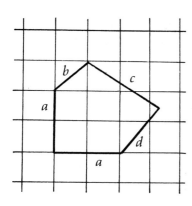

$$p = a + a + b + c + d$$

or

$$p = 2a + b + c + d$$

7 Writing formulae

Ask the children to invent formulae for specific situations, for example, the cost of a number of ice-creams at 15p each. Let the total cost be c (pence). Let the number bought be n (number). So the total cost is

$$c = 15n \text{ (pence)}$$

Discuss what is meant by $15n$, i.e. 15 lots of n or $15 \times n$. Explain that the '$\times$' sign is not needed when using letters.

Give the children values for n and ask them to find the value of c.

8 Another formula

Remind the children about the relationship between faces, vertices and edges of solid shapes:

$$F + V = E + 2$$

Give them practice in investigating solid shapes to demonstrate the formula.

9 Area of a circle

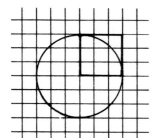

You could develop the work on formulae by asking the children to draw a circle on squared paper and find its area by counting squares. Then ask them to find the area of the radius of the circle squared.

Do they notice that the area of the whole circle is always about 3 times that of the radius squared? Can they write a formula for this:

$$A = 3r^2 ?$$

This will eventually lead to $A = \pi r^2$,

Can they use the area of a circle to write the volume of a cylinder?

$$V = 3r^2h \text{ (approximately)}$$
or $V = \pi r^2 h$

MENTAL WORK Show the children simple formulae, for example,

$$p = 4a$$

and ask them to find p when given the value for a, such as $a = 2$.

LINKS WITH THE ENVIRONMENT Talk with the children about when we might use formulae in everyday life. For example:

$$A = L \times W = LW \quad \text{(For the area of a rectangle)}$$
$$V = L \times W \times H = LWH \quad \text{(for the volume of a cuboid)}$$

Discuss what the letters stand for.

NOTES ON
INVESTIGATIONS

Section A

Do the children choose a value for the area that has a number of factors and then use the formula $A = L \times W$? Do they devise a logical way of recording their results, such as a chart?

L	W	A
48 cm	1 cm	48 cm²
24 cm	2 cm	48 cm²
16 cm	3 cm	48 cm²
12 cm	4 cm	48 cm²
8 cm	6 cm	48 cm²

Section B

Do the children deduce that the formula $p = 3a + 2b$ could apply to a closed shape of five sides where three sides (of length a) are the same and the two other sides (of length b) are the same as each other but different to a? For example:

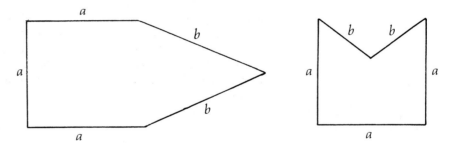

Section C

Do the children realise that the area of a square of side a is $a \times a = a^2$? Do they use a trial and improvement method, using a calculator to solve $a \times a = 3$? For example:

$$\begin{aligned}
1 \times \quad 1 &= 1 \quad \text{(too small)} \\
2 \times \quad 2 &= 4 \quad \text{(too large)} \\
1{\cdot}5 \times \quad 1{\cdot}5 &= 2{\cdot}25 \text{ (too small)} \\
1{\cdot}75 \times 1{\cdot}75 &= 3{\cdot}06 \text{ (too large)}
\end{aligned}$$

Note that $\sqrt{3} \approx 1{\cdot}732$.

Angles 2

Purpose

- To revise horizontal, vertical, perpendicular and parallel lines
- To revise tessellations
- To revise measuring angles to 5°
- To introduce measuring angles to 1°
- To construct simple two-dimensional shapes from given information
- To identify equal angles in a diagram
- To use angle properties of two-dimensional shapes to determine whether a tessellation of given shapes is possible

Materials

Rulers, protractor, templates (edge-matched equilateral triangle, square, regular hexagon, regular octagon), card, tracing paper

Vocabulary

Vertical, perpendicular, horizontal, parallel, correct, parallel sides, pair, measure, acute, obtuse, reflex, right angle, quadrilateral, pentagon, triangle, lettered angle, side, equal, centre, template, square, regular hexagon, regular octagon, patterns, angles at a point, design, tessellate, measurements, missing angle, identical, diagonal, divide, sum

TEACHING POINTS   SECTION A

1 Horizontal and vertical

Talk with the children about the words 'horizontal' and 'vertical'. They may have heard the words before in gymnastics – vertical rings, horizontal bars or horizontal beam. Ask a child to stand vertically and another to lie horizontally. Point out the relationship with the horizon.

Ask a group of children to each name something in the room that is horizontal and another group to each name something that is vertical. Examples might include the floor, window-sill, table tops, the board, the walls.

Show the children a plumb bob and ask whether the line it makes is vertical or horizontal. Explain how a spirit level works. Ask what might happen if buildings were made without using equipment which measures horizontal and vertical. Can they think of a building which is not vertical? (The Leaning Tower of Pisa.)

plumb bob

Ask them to draw some lines to represent horizontal and vertical. Although vertical is at right angles to the horizon, it is often represented as a line going to the top of the paper.

2 Perpendicular

Talk about the word 'perpendicular' and explain how it can be related to horizontal and vertical. Ask the children to fold a piece of paper into a right angle or square corner. Explain that if lines or objects are perpendicular to each other the square corner or right angle should fit exactly. What do they notice about horizontal and vertical objects? (They are at right angles.)

Draw pairs of intersecting lines, some of which meet at right angles. Ask the children to find which lines are perpendicular to each other.

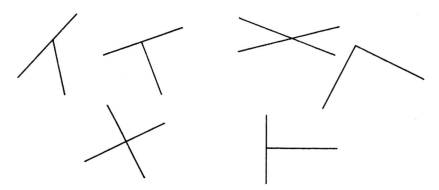

Point out that lines can be perpendicular without necessarily being horizontal and vertical.

3 Parallel lines

Talk about parallel lines and remind the children that these are sets of lines which are the same distance apart for the whole of their length and are often different lengths. Arrows are used to show that lines are parallel.

Can the children find any parallel lines in the classroom or the environment? Examples are opposite sides of a table, walls, window frames, fence posts.

Let the children draw some parallel lines on squared paper or by using a ruler.

You might wish to discuss examples of parallel lines in the environment such as the opposite sides of a road or railway lines.

4 Naming lines

Draw some intersecting lines. Ask the children to name the types of line, using their folded square corner when necessary.

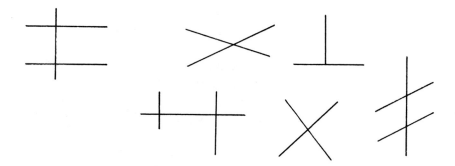

Let them use squared paper to draw some intersecting lines and ask a friend to name properties – for example, vertical, horizontal, parallel, perpendicular.

A game to play

NAME THE LINES

The first child in a team draws a shape which has at least one example of horizontal, vertical, perpendicular or parallel lines.

A child from the second team scores 1 point for each correct name for the types of lines shown. The teams then change over. The first to score 12 points is the winner.

Talk about the names of the shapes drawn during 'Name the lines'. The names of different quadrilaterals are needed for the section A investigation. Do the children appreciate that pentagons, for example, do not need to have all sides the same length? Regular pentagons have all sides and angles equal.

5 Angles

Revise the fact that there are 360° in a circle. Fold a paper circle into quarters and ask how many degrees there are in a right angle.

6 Acute, obtuse and reflex angles

Remind the children about acute, obtuse and reflex angles.

7 Measuring angles to 5°

Talk about measuring angles. A variety of protractors are available for schools. A useful model is the SMP angle measurer.

Give the children practice in both drawing and measuring acute, obtuse and reflex angles to 5° with the protractors you use. Can they name the angles they draw and measure?

A game to play

NEAREST ESTIMATE

Play the game in groups of two, three or four.

The first child draws an angle accurately to 5° on a piece of paper. The angle is shown to the rest of the group who each have to estimate the angle to the nearest 5°. The estimate nearest to the true measurement scores 1 point. The children take turns to draw an angle. The winner is the first to score 5 points.

8 Revise tessellations

Talk about tessellating shapes that fit together without overlapping or leaving gaps. Can the children see any tessellating shapes in the classroom such as floor tiles, ceiling tiles, wired glass in doors etc.?

Ask the children to name some shapes that they think will tessellate and others that will not. Record the children's answers in a table.

These shapes will tessellate	These shapes will not tessellate
square rectangle equilateral triangle regular hexagon	circle regular pentagon regular octagon

Ask the children to choose a template of one of the shapes and draw round it several times to show whether it will or will not tessellate. Can the children name any shapes which they have seen tessellating together in tiling patterns or patchwork? For example, equilateral triangles and squares. The angles at a point add up to 360°.

This work is developed in the pupils' book. (See also Shape 4, Module 6.)

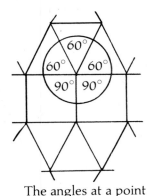

The angles at a point add up to 360°.

SECTION B AND C

9 Measuring and drawing angles to 1°

Talk about measuring angles accurately to 1° using a protractor or angle measurer. Give the children practice in drawing angles to 1°. Remind them that pencils need to be sharpened for accuracy.

10 Constructing triangles

Talk with the children about constructing two-dimensional shapes using ruler, protractor and compass. Ask them to construct an equilateral triangle whose sides are 10 cm long. Ask them to measure each angle. Talk about the different methods. Three ways are as follows.

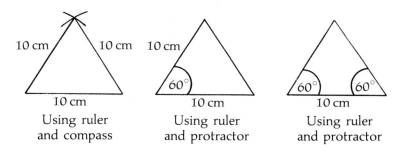

| Using ruler and compass | Using ruler and protractor | Using ruler and protractor |

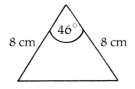

Ask them to construct an isosceles triangle. Talk about their methods of construction. Ask them to measure the missing angles.

   The children are asked to construct scalene triangles in the pupils' book.

11 Quadrilaterals

Talk about the different types of quadrilaterals and their definitions (see the glossary).

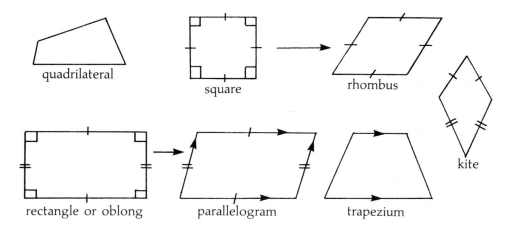

Ask the children to construct some using ruler, compass and protractor. Can they measure the angles accurately? Which angles are equal? Why?

The children are asked to construct a quadrilateral in the pupils' book.

12 Regular shapes

You might wish to talk about constructing regular shapes using rulers, compasses and protractors. Ask the children first to find a way to calculate the angles and construct some shapes.

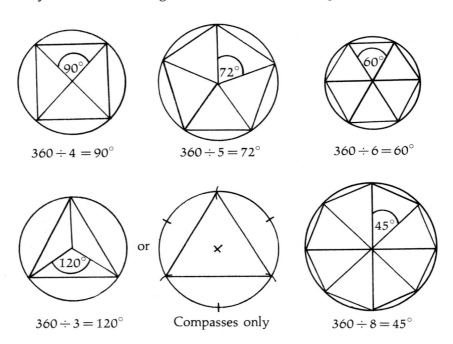

$360 \div 4 = 90°$ $360 \div 5 = 72°$ $360 \div 6 = 60°$

$360 \div 3 = 120°$ or   Compasses only $360 \div 8 = 45°$

13 Logo

Discuss how shapes and angles can be drawn using Turtle graphics. Set the children problems to draw using Logo or let them devise their own.

14 Tessellating triangles

Ask the children to use a triangle template or construct one from card. Let them draw and cut out six identical triangles from paper. Mark the angles a, b, c on each triangle. Can they make their six triangles tessellate without turning them over? The triangles must be rotated until the angles $a + b + c + a + b + c$ come together.

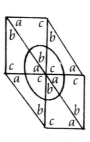

right angled

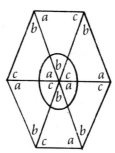

isosceles

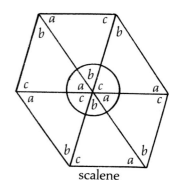

scalene

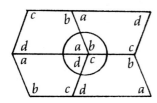

What do the angle sums add up to? (Two sets of three angles $(a+b+c)$ together add up to 360°.)

The children are asked to tessellate quadrilaterals in a similar way in the pupils' book. In this case the angle sum is $a+b+c+d=360°$.

LINKS WITH THE ENVIRONMENT

Talk about everyday situations involving angles and tessellations.

- Buildings – look for acute and obtuse angles in buildings. Windows can show tessellations, tiles around swimming baths, mosaic pictures, brick patterns.
- Art and craft – look at pattern work in art and model making.
- PE – make angles with arms and legs. Look at the large climbing apparatus for angles.
- A children's playground in a park – look at the angles made by the fixing poles of swings, roundabouts and climbing frames. Ask the children to look for tessellations as they come to school. Examples might include paving stones, zebra crossing, shopping precinct floors.
- Some boxes in supermarkets tessellate.
- Wallpaper, wrapping paper, tile, fabric and knitting designs can show tessellating patterns.

NOTES ON INVESTIGATIONS

Section A

Do the children's quadrilaterals always have two pairs of parallel sides? For example:

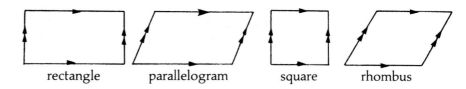

rectangle   parallelogram   square   rhombus

Do the children appreciate that pentagons need not be regular? Do they realise that pentagons can have either one pair or two pairs of parallel lines?

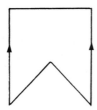 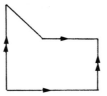

Do they find that different hexagons can have one pair, two pairs or three pairs of parallel lines? For example:

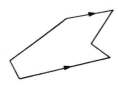 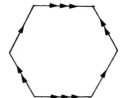 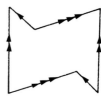

Section B

Do the children notice that the angles of the four small triangles are all the same, and are equal to the angles of the large triangle? They may notice that the angle sum of each triangle is 180° and the angle sum at the centre of each side is 180°. Do they come to realise that this will work for any triangle?

Section C

The children will find that $a+b+c+d+e+f=360°$. Dividing a quadrilateral into two triangles (each of whose angles add up to 180°) shows that the angles of the quadrilateral total 360°, i.e. $180° + 180° = 360°$.

Number 7

Purpose

- To revise place value and rounding large numbers
- To introduce index notation
- To use trial and improvement methods
- To introduce approximation, using significant figures
- To give practice in generating sequences

Materials

Calculator, squared paper

Vocabulary

Difference, diameter, round, rounded, digits, predict, pattern, approximately, significant figures, estimate, million, thousand thousands, double, minimum, cube, total, constant difference

TEACHING POINTS   **SECTION A**

1 Revising place value

Talk with the children about place value and how the first digit of a number gives the best indication of its size; for example, **2**147 (the '2' is worth 2000) or **1**2 147 (the '1' is worth 10 000).

Write a set of numbers (these may be distances) and ask the children to put them in order of size.

A game to play

MAKING NUMBERS

Make two sets of cards, one set marked 1 to 9 (with several of each), and another set marked tens , hundreds , thousands (several of each). The two sets of cards are each shuffled and placed face downwards on the table. Hold up one card from each pack, for example,

Children then have to write a four-digit number with '7' in the hundreds column, for example, 3758.

2 Rounding

Give the children practice in rounding numbers to the nearest 10, 100, 1000. Remind them that the numbers may round up or down.

$17 \rightarrow 20$ (nearest 10) $4256 \rightarrow 4000$ (nearest 1000)
$145 \rightarrow 100$ (nearest 100) $987 \rightarrow 1000$ (nearest 1000)
$13\,240 \rightarrow 13\,000$ (nearest 1000)

A game to play

ROUND THEM

Make a set of cards showing four-digit numbers (for example, 3724 , 1256 , etc.) and another set showing ten hundred thousand (several of each). Shuffle each pack and place them face downwards on the table. Hold up one card from each pack. The children have to rewrite the number, rounding it as shown. For example:

	Round to nearest	
3724	hundred	3700
1256	ten	1260

SECTIONS B AND C

3 Index notation

Show the children a 'short' way of writing $2 \times 2 \times 2 \times 2 \times 2$; that is 2^5.
Ask what they think 2^3 would be worth.
Use a calculator to demonstrate the value of

$$2^4 = 2 \times 2 \times 2 \times 2 = 16$$

Ask the children to write out and find values for 3^2, 4^3, 5^4, using a calculator if they wish.

A game to play

REWRITE IT

Hold up flash cards such as 2^3 , 3^4 , etc. children have to rewrite the numbers, using the multiplication sign, for example,

$$3 \times 3 \times 3 \times 3$$

4 Trial and improvement

Give the children a 'puzzle', $\Box^2 = 196$. Discuss how this could be written

$$\triangle \times \triangle = 196$$

Ask them to suggest a number and discuss whether it is too large or too small. For example, if 8 is suggested:

'$8 \times 8 = 64$. Too small, try a much larger number. What about 16?'
'$16 \times 16 = 256$. Too big now but we are closer. What shall we try now?'

Carry on discussion of this type until the correct answer of 14 is arrived at. Encourage the children to develop a logical improvement technique, not just guesswork.

5 Significant figures

Explain that as well as rounding to tens, hundreds, thousands, etc., we can also round to the most significant or important figures. For example, in 1734 the most significant figure is the 1 as it is worth the most, i.e. 1000. The second most significant figure is the 7 as it has the next highest value. So if we round 1734 to two significant figures it rounds down to 1700 (as 3 is less than 5). Note that 1754 would round up to 1800.

A game to play

MACHINE

Invent a function machine that rounds to two significant figures.

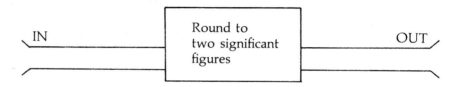

Make a set of cards to go 'IN'. For example,

Hold one of the cards in position at the 'IN' of the machine and give the children a set time to record the 'IN' and 'OUT' numbers.

Round to two significant figures	
IN	OUT
1869	1900
14 834	15 000

MENTAL WORK Give the children mental 'puzzles' involving patterns. Can they recognise how the patterns are developed? For example:

24   35   46   57   68   79   90

Explain that the difference between each number in the pattern often helps to work out the next number in the pattern. For example:

$$24 \quad 35 \quad 46 \quad 57$$
difference $\quad\quad 11 \quad 11 \quad 11$

Explain that if the difference is the same each time, it is called the constant difference.

USING THE CALCULATOR

- Remind the children about the constant function on their calculators. Give them practice in using it to show the constant difference in number patterns. For example:

  $117 \rightarrow 108 \rightarrow 99 \rightarrow 90 \rightarrow$ etc.   (subtracting 9)
  $132 \rightarrow 120 \rightarrow 108 \rightarrow$ etc.   (subtracting 12)

  Can the children predict the patterns?
- Give the children practice in developing other number patterns and in generating sequences. For example:

  3 $\boxed{+}$ $\boxed{+}$ 9 $\rightarrow$ 12 21 30 etc. (calculators may vary.)

- Let the children use the constant function to resolve index notation problems, for example, 3 $\boxed{\times}$ $\boxed{\times}$ to resolve 3^4.

LINKS WITH THE ENVIRONMENT

Talk with the children about when they might read or see large numbers.

- Distances in the Solar System
- Distances recorded on car mileometers
- Numbers of people living in large cities, countries, the world
- Distances of rivers and heights of mountains

NOTES ON INVESTIGATIONS

Section A

Are the children innovative in their ideas? As well as merely entering 1 000 000 on their calculator, do they include such solutions as

$10 \times 10 \times 10 \times 10 \times 10 \times 10 = 1\,000\,000$ $\quad$ $100 \times 100 \times 100 = 1\,000\,000$
$1000 \times 1000 = 1\,000\,000$ $\quad\quad\quad\quad\quad\quad$ $100\,000 \times 10 = 1\,000\,000$
$10\,000 \times 100 = 1\,000\,000$ $\quad\quad\quad\quad\quad\quad$ $100 \times 10\,000 = 1\,000\,000$
$10 \times 100\,000 = 1\,000\,000$ $\quad\quad\quad\quad\quad$ $500\,000 \times 2 = 1\,000\,000$

etc.?

Section B

Do the children realise that the total must lie between 1750 and 1849 (inclusive) if it is to be 1800 when rounded to 2 significant figures? Obviously, there are many pairs of numbers that can be suggested.

Similarly, the second total must lie between 1985 and 1994 (inclusive) if it is to be 1990 when rounded to 3 significant figures. Again, there are many possible answers.

Section C

Do the children suggest more than one way of completing the pattern? For example,

    1   2   4   8   16   32   64 . . . (doubling each time)
    1   2   4   7   11   16   22 . . . (add 1, add 2, add 3 etc.)

Are the children able to explain their rules for generating the sequences?

Measurement 2

Purpose

- To revise measurement
- To give practice in estimating measurement
- To give experience in the use of imperial units and their metric equivalents

Materials

Timer or stop watch, pack of playing cards, counters, tape measures, height measure, metre stick, orange, tin of baked beans, tie, various jugs and containers (see pupils' book), capacity jugs or measurers, objects for weighing, paper labels for matching, weighing scales, bathroom scales, rulers, thermometer, centimetre squared paper, car brochures and magazines

Vocabulary

Slower, quicker, estimated time, measurements, metres, centimetres, circumference, length, average, height, closest, estimates, litre, millilitre (ml), measuring jug, container, pairs, 'odd one out', match, weigh, weight, label, correct match, bathroom scales, record, twice, chart, diagram, measures, kilograms, grams, imperial units, metric units, ounces (oz), pounds (lb), liquid, pints, gallons, approximately, miles, Mini, kilometres, inches (in), feet (ft), yards (yd), information, straight line graph, suitable scale, distance, speed limits, per hour, temperature, degrees Celsius (Centigrade), degrees Fahrenheit, freezing and boiling points, nearest °F, nearest °C, normal body temperature, equivalent

TEACHING POINTS   SECTION A

1 Timing in minutes and seconds

Talk about occasions when it is necessary to time events accurately such as when cooking and in sporting events. Remind the children how to use the timing devices available in school such as stop watches and clocks, tockers, etc.

2 Estimating time

Can the children estimate the length of 1 minute, 30 seconds, 10 seconds? Can they count seconds?

Set simple tasks for them to estimate and then time how long it takes to do them. For example, how long will it take them to write the numbers 1 to 30? How many words can they read aloud in $\frac{1}{2}$ minute?

A game to play

ESTIMATES

This game is for two or more groups.

Give the groups an activity to do such as write the alphabet. Each group estimates the time, in seconds, that it will take to do the activity. They write this estimate down. They then choose one member of the group to do the activity and they time them. The group making the closest estimate is the winner.

3 Weight, capacity and length

Remind the children of the metric units for these measures. Talk about the full and abbreviated name for each one. Ask them to make charts or mobiles.

The children might be interested to know that 'milli' means one thousandth, from the Latin word *'mille'* meaning a thousand. What do they notice about millimetre and millilitre? 'Kilo' is from the

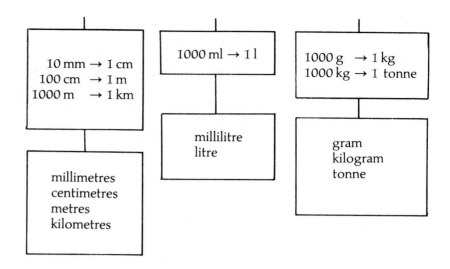

Greek word *'chilioi'* meaning one thousand, and 'centi' from the Latin word *'centum'*, meaning one hundred. What do the children notice about kilograms and centimetres?

4 Notation

Remind the children of the notation of metric measures.

$$1·25 \text{ m} \rightarrow 125 \text{ cm}$$
$$1·250 \text{ km} \rightarrow 1250 \text{ m}$$
$$1·250 \text{ l} \rightarrow 1250 \text{ ml etc.}$$

Give them practice in changing measurements from one unit to another. Remind them that 2·500 l can be written as 2·5 l, and 2·250 l as 2·25 l.

5 Measuring

Give the children revision practice in estimating and measuring length, weight and capacity. Can they find objects that only measure a small number of g, ml, or cm?

Ask them to find some average measurements to the nearest centimetre or kilogram, for example, their average stride or standing jump, and the average height and weight of five friends. (A calculator may be useful.)

A game to play

ESTIMATE THE LENGTH

This game is for two or more groups.

Ask the groups to estimate a length to the nearest metre, for example, the length of 20 strides. They then measure the length and compare it with their estimate. They score points as follows: 3 points for a correct estimate; 1 point for an estimate which is only 1 length more or less than the true measurement.

The activity can be repeated, estimating and measuring other lengths, such as the length of a PE bench, a corridor, etc.

The winning group is the one with the highest score.

SECTIONS B AND C

6 Imperial units

Talk to the children about the many different units of imperial measurement and how they derive from different origins. Many units of length were based on parts of the body,

- The mile was the Roman 'milia' or thousand paces.
- The yard was the distance from the chin to the fingertips when the arm was outstretched.
- The inch was approximately the width of a man's thumb. (Inch is from the Latin 'uncia' meaning 12th part, hence 12 inches = 1 foot.)
- The foot was the length of a man's foot.

Talk about the problems of using arbitrary measurements such as these, how they vary from person to person. As trade developed over the centuries, several kings tried to standardise the measurements. It is said that Henry I decreed that the yard was to be the length from his chin to his fingertips. Over the years many units of measurement became standardised by law and became known as imperial units.

7 Measurement tables

Write tables showing imperial units and talk about them.

12 inches (in)	→ 1 foot
3 feet (ft)	→ 1 yard (yd)
36 inches	→ 1 yard
22 yards	→ 1 chain
10 chains	→ 1 furlong
8 furlongs	→ 1 mile
1760 yards	→ 1 mile
2 pints	→ 1 quart
4 quarts	→ 1 gallon
8 pints	→ 1 gallon
16 ounces (oz)	→ 1 pound (1 lb)
14 pounds	→ 1 stone
8 stones	→ 1 hundredweight (cwt)
20 hundredweights	→ 1 ton

Some of these measurements are still used in shops and market stalls, for example,

yards of ribbon, material, $\frac{1}{2}$ lb of cheese.

Talk about how much more difficult it is to calculate using imperial measurements. Give them some to try, for example:

yd	ft	ins		stones	lb	oz		lb	oz
2	2	9		10	4	9		12	8
+1	2	11		+ 4	12	8		− 6	9
				1	7	12			

Did their parents or grandparents use imperial measurements at school?

A game to play

IMPERIAL LENGTH

This game is for two or more groups.
    Give each group a set of five flash cards of length measurements.

8 furlongs = 1 mile		12 in = 1 foot

10 chains = 1 furlong	22 yd = 1 chain	3 feet = 1 yard

Ask them to shuffle the cards and put them in order as quickly as possible. The first group to do so is the winner.

8 Practical work

Give the children some experience in using imperial measurement. For example:

- What is their weight in stones and lbs?
- What is their height in feet and inches?
- Weigh $\frac{1}{4}$ lb of marbles or nails.

9 The metric system

Talk about how the metric system developed and how it became law in France in 1795. It became popular in most European countries but Britain did not adopt it then because they were at war with France. Britain started using a metric or decimal system when the currency system was changed on 15 February 1971. The metric system of weights and measures was adopted in the UK from 1975.

Look at the metric tables.

$$10\,\text{mm} \to 1\,\text{cm}$$
$$100\,\text{cm} \to 1\,\text{m}$$
$$1000\,\text{m} \to 1\,\text{km}$$

Do the children notice that they are based on units of 10? How does this compare with the imperial system for solving measurement problems?

$$250\,\text{g} = \square\,\text{kg} \qquad 248\,\text{oz} = \square\,\text{lb}\ \square\,\text{oz}$$

They might be interested to know that length, weight and capacity were all linked in the metric system. A cube of edge $\frac{1}{10}$ metre holds 1 litre of water which weighs 1 kilogram.

Explain that it is much easier to use a common system of measurement, such as the metric system, when countries are trading and working together. For example:

- Car parts made in Britain are sold in Germany.
- Concorde was built in France and in Britain.
- The Channel tunnel was built from France and England and joined up under the English Channel.

10 Temperature

Talk with the children about thermometers and their scales, how temperatures can be measured in degrees Celsius (centigrade) or Fahrenheit. Which is most commonly used today? Can they tell you the boiling and freezing points for each scale?

They might be interested to know the origins of the two scales. The Fahrenheit scale was invented by D. G. Fahrenheit (1686–1736), a German physicist, and the Celsius scale was named after the Swedish scientist Anders Celsius (1701–1744).

Do the children know what their normal body temperature is in °F and °C (about 98·4 °F or 37 °C)? On a hot day when the temperature is in the 70s, is this Celsius or Fahrenheit?

MENTAL WORK

- Ask the children to work out simple measurement fractions, for example, $\frac{1}{4}, \frac{1}{2}, \frac{3}{4}$ of a litre, kilogram, kilometre, metre.
- Give the children practice in completing number patterns.

33, 38, 43, ____ ____ ____ ____ ____ ____ ____
24, 32, 40, ____ ____ ____ ____ ____ ____ ____
122, 102, 82, ____ ____ ____ ____ ____ ____

- Give simple word problems about the measurement tables.

How many ml in 2·5 litres? How many g in 3·5 kg?
How many feet in a yard?
How many inches long would a yard of ribbon be?

A game to play

JUMBLED UP

This game can be played by two or more groups of children.
Make a set of matching cards using metric measures, for example:

$\frac{1}{2}$ l	500 ml	$\frac{1}{2}$ m	50 cm	$\frac{1}{2}$ kg	500 g
$\frac{1}{4}$ l	250 ml	$\frac{1}{4}$ m	25 cm	$\frac{1}{4}$ kg	250 g
$\frac{3}{4}$ l	750 ml	$\frac{3}{4}$ m	75 cm	$\frac{3}{4}$ kg	750 g
1 l	1000 ml	1 m	100 cm	1 kg	1000 g

Give each group an identical set to shuffle. At a given signal each
group pairs the cards as quickly as possible. The first group to do so
correctly is the winner.
   This game could be repeated using sets of matching cards
showing imperial measurements.

**USING THE
CALCULATOR**
Talk with the children about the need to know more difficult
multiplication tables when calculating imperial measurements. Can
they build up their 12, 14, 16 multiplication tables?
   • Ask simple questions about imperial units such as:

How many pounds in 2 stones?
How many pounds in 1 cwt?

   • Give the children practice in building number patterns related
     to metric measurements such as counting in 200s, 250s, 500s.

**LINKS WITH THE
ENVIRONMENT**
Talk about everyday situations involving measurement.
   • Buying food – cheese, bacon, meat, vegetables
   • Tinned and bottled foods – gross and net weights
   • Buying pet food – oats, pellets, etc.
   • Weighing luggage at airports, lorries on weigh-bridges, babies,
     jockeys, etc.

- Weighing money in banks — compare the weights of new/old coins
- The capacity of drink containers — bottles, cans, cartons
- The amount of water used when we use a washing machine, take a shower, flush the toilet
- Buying material, ribbon, wood, wire, by the length
- The measurements of clothes and shoes
- Body temperature, the temperature of the classroom, the national temperature shown on the weather forecast, the world temperature shown in newspapers
- Record times for races in athletics, or other sporting events
- Timing everyday things, for example, boiling an egg
- Measuring distances on maps, speedometers, mileometers

Talk about things that we measure in metric measurements, e.g. lemonade, and things that are often still measured in imperial units, e.g. bottles of milk. Although many lengths are measured metrically now, the mile is still the unit used in Britain for measuring long distances, unlike France, for example, which measure long distances in kilometres.

NOTES ON INVESTIGATIONS

Section A

Do the children devise an interesting list of 'personal' measurements, which include units of time, weight, length, capacity, etc.? Possibilities are the time it takes them to walk to school, how far they can run in 15 seconds, how high they can jump, how much liquid they drink in a day, how hard they can press down on bathroom scales.

Section B

Do the children understand both the imperial and metric systems? Do they recognise the different systems when they see measurements marked on objects? For example, do they recognise miles as part of the imperial system and kilometres as part of the metric system?

Imperial	Metric
miles on motorway pints of milk gallons of petrol etc.	litres of cola kilogram of sugar etc.

Section C

Do the children use car brochures and magazines to check the data? Are they able to convert miles per gallon into kilometres per litre? (Note: many car brochures give fuel consumption in terms of litres per 100 kilometres, rather than kilometres per litre.)

Number 8

Purpose

- To revise division bonds
- To revise division by one digit
- To introduce division of two digits by two digits, and three digits by two digits

Materials

Dice, name cards (see pupils' book), squared paper, calculator

Vocabulary

Division, share equally, average, re-arrange, answers, inside circle, dice, score, divide exactly, point, remainder, estimate, exact answer, method, clearly divided, cross-number puzzle, shuffle, division problem, question, accurately, calculator, difference between, accurate answer, estimated answer, highest total score, result

TEACHING POINTS   SECTION A

1 Division patterns

Revise grouping numbers into patterns of 4, 6, 7, 8, 9, etc. Ask questions which emphasise the link between division and multiplication. For example:

$$56 \div 8 = \square$$
$$\square \times 8 = 56$$

What are two sevens?
How many sevens in fourteen?
How many different number sentences can you make using 9, 7, 63, $\times$, $\div$, $=$?

Ask the children to make up similar questions for friends to answer.

Give them practice in using multiplication to check the answers to division problems, for example,

$$40 \div 8 = 5 \qquad 5 \times 8 = 40$$

2 Division bonds

Revise multiplication tables. Give the children practice in using them to solve simple division problems. For example:

$$42 \div 7 = \square \qquad 42 \div \square = 7 \qquad \square \div 7 = 6$$

Ask questions such as:

How can I get an answer of 3 by dividing?

$$\square \div \square = 3$$

What is the missing number?

$$48 \div 8 \div 2 = \square$$

3 Rules for divisibility

Talk with the children about the rules for divisibility. How many can they remember?

- Divisible by 2 – numbers end in 2, 4, 6, 8, 0
- Divisible by 3 – the digit sum of the number is divisible by 3
- Divisible by 5 – numbers end in 5 and 0
- Divisible by 10 – numbers end in 0

Encourage them to explain the rules to their classmates and give examples. The other children can check the divisibility on their calculators.

A game to play

SORT THEM

This game is for any number of children.

Write a selection of related numbers on the board and ask the children to sort them into divisibility groups. Which is the odd one out? The first child to find it is the winner.

$$24 \qquad 18 \qquad 27 \qquad 36$$
$$21 \qquad 27 \qquad 30 \qquad 40 \qquad 42$$
$$25 \qquad 31 \qquad 35$$

The game can be extended by using bigger numbers or by finding numbers which fit into more than one divisibility group.

4 Recording and solving problems

Ask the children to suggest different methods of recording divisions. For example:

Divide 152 by 4   4$\overline{)152}$ 4$\overline{)152}$

$152 \div 4$ $\frac{152}{4}$

Talk about solving division problems. Can the children suggest different methods?

$$
\begin{array}{c}
33\ r2 \\
4\overline{)134}
\end{array}
\quad \text{or} \quad
\begin{array}{l}
20 \rightarrow 33\ r2 \\
4\overline{)134} \\
80 \leftarrow 20 \times 4 \\
\overline{54} \\
40 \leftarrow 10 \times 4 \\
\overline{14} \\
12 \leftarrow 3 \times 4 \\
\overline{2}
\end{array}
\quad \text{or} \quad
\begin{array}{c}
33\ r2 \\
4\overline{)134} \\
12 \\
\overline{14} \\
12 \\
\overline{2}
\end{array}
$$

Talk about how practical these methods are and which one they prefer to use.

Give the children practice in dividing two-, three-, and four-digit numbers by one digit, including exchanging or 'carrying', and remainders. Include some examples where an answer includes '0'.

$$
\begin{array}{c}
208\ r1 \\
4\overline{)833}
\end{array}
\qquad
\begin{array}{c}
302\ r2 \\
3\overline{)908}
\end{array}
\qquad
\begin{array}{c}
60\ r5 \\
6\overline{)365}
\end{array}
$$

A game to play

REMAINDERS

This game is for two teams.
Give the children a remainder, for example, 4. A player from each team has to write a division problem on the board which will give a remainder of 4, such as

$49 \div 5 = 9\ r4$

The first player to do so scores a point for their team. The winning team is the one with the highest score at the end of the round.

5 Further practice in division

Make up a simple cross-number puzzle using division problems

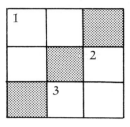

Across	Down
1 $48 \div 2$	**1** $66 \div 3$
3 $44 \div 4$	**2** $\square \div 7 = 3$

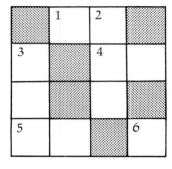

Ask the children to make up their own cross-number puzzles involving division. The format of the puzzle can obviously be developed according to the capabilities of the children. A calculator will be very useful for checking the answers to the harder clues.

Give the children a magic square to copy and solve

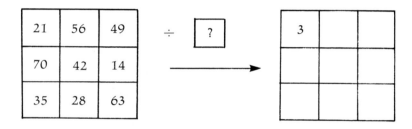

What is the total for each row, column, diagonal? Do they notice that they are the same totals? Can they make another magic square involving division based on the one you gave them?

6 Verbal problems

Give the children practice in solving word problems. For example:

> There were 112 children at the school party. They sat at tables of 8. How many tables were needed?

Talk about knowing when to multiply or divide in order to solve a problem, and how it helps to know if the answer is likely to be bigger or smaller than the starting number. Give them more practice in solving word problems bearing this in mind. Can they devise any problems themselves?

SECTIONS B AND C

7 Division of two- and three-digit numbers by two digits

Talk with the children about occasions when it might be necessary to divide a two- or three-digit number by a two-digit one – for example, when finding the average size of family for the children in the class.

8 Division by 10, 20, etc.

Give the children practice in dividing by tens on their calculators. Can they explain what happens? Can they predict answers and then check them on their calculators?

9 Solving division problems

Write a problem on the board.

$174 \div 14$

Ask the children to suggest ways of solving it, other than by using a calculator. Write their suggestions on the board. Two possible methods are

```
      12 r6
  14)174              14)174
      14                  140  ← 14 × 10
      ──                  ───
      34                   34
      28                   28  ← 14 × 2
      ──                   ──
       6                    6         12 r6
```

Talk with the children about their suggested methods and the possible advantages and disadvantages of each one. Let them choose the method they prefer and give them practice in using it, dividing by numbers between 11 and 20 to begin with. The children could build up some of the tables for these numbers on their calculators.

$1 \times 16 = 16$
$2 \times 16 = 32$ etc.

10 Estimation

Talk about how useful it is to estimate the answer first, by rounding.

$82 \div 18 \rightarrow 80 \div 20 \rightarrow 4$

This may give the correct answer, or an indication of whether to try a larger or smaller number using a trial and improvement technique. Give the children practice in this, dividing two digits by two digits to begin with.

Games to play

DIVIDE BY TENS AND HUNDREDS

This game is for two or more groups.
Make pairs of cards, one with a division problem and the other with the answer.

| $600 \div 10$ | 60 | $800 \div 20$ | 40 | $800 \div 100$ | 8 |

Each group has an identical set of cards which they shuffle. At a given signal the groups have to match the problems to the answers. The first group to match them all correctly is the winner.

MATCH THE REMAINDERS

This game is similar to the previous one. This time write some division problems on the board and write their remainders separately, but not in the same order.

$46 \div 14$ Rem 1
$62 \div 15$ Rem 2
$42 \div 13$ Rem 3
$49 \div 12$ Rem 4
$60 \div 11$ Rem 5

The groups have to match the remainder to its problem as quickly as possible. The first group to do so correctly wins.

MENTAL WORK

- Give the children practice in using division and multiplication bonds up to 10×10, $100 \div 10$.
- Give them practice in dividing exactly by 10s, 20s, etc.

$400 \div 10$, $440 \div 10$
$400 \div 20$, $440 \div 20$

- Ask them to find the remainder for division problems.

$66 \div 8$. What is the remainder?

- Ask them to make up problems with a specific remainder.
- Ask them to write two- or three-digit numbers which are divisible by 3. Do the same for the other rules of divisibility.
- Ask them to solve division problems written like this:

$\frac{42}{6}$

- Ask verbal problems such as:

How many children could share 54 sweets and get 6 each?
If 38 children are put into 4 teams, how many extra children will there be?

USING THE CALCULATOR

Remind the children that if the number does not divide exactly on the calculator there are numbers after the decimal point; that is, the answer is not a whole number. Give them practice in finding numbers that divide exactly and those that don't.

Ask them to suggest larger numbers that will divide exactly by 2, 3, 5, or 9, for example $4221 \div 3$. They can then check their suggestions on their calculators.

Let them investigate division by 10, 20, 30, etc. with larger numbers. What do they notice?

LINKS WITH THE ENVIRONMENT

- Finding averages when larger numbers are involved
- Sharing equipment between a large number of children
- Organising rows of chairs for a concert, tables for a school party, number of coaches needed for a school outing

NOTES ON INVESTIGATIONS

Section A

The children could first find one three-digit number that is exactly divisible by 7, perhaps by counting on in 7s on a calculator (. . ., 70, 77, 84, 91, 98, **105**). They could then find more numbers by adding on 7 each time: 105, 112, 119. The same technique can be used to find numbers that divide by 8, and then add 3 each time.

Section B

Do the children devise a method to make up problems? One way is as follows: if you are devising a problem dividing by 22 and 25, write down the multiples of the numbers 22 and 25, choose a number and work out the appropriate remainders. For example:

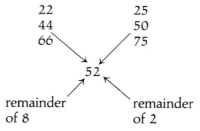

In the above case the number 52 has a remainder of 8 when divided by 22 and a remainder of 2 when divided by 25.

Section C

Do the children realise that the smallest two-digit number is 10? Do they then work logically through larger two-digit numbers until they exhaust all the appropriate three-digit numbers? They could use multiplication as the inverse of division to find the answers.

Two-digit number		Three-digit number	
10	10×50	500	$500 \div 10 = 50$
11	11×50	550	$550 \div 11 = 50$
12	12×50	600	$600 \div 12 = 50$
$\vdots$	$\vdots$	$\vdots$	$\vdots$
19	19×50	950	$950 \div 19 = 50$

shape 2

Purpose

- To revise reflective and rotational symmetry
- To revise planes of symmetry
- To investigate centres, axes and planes of symmetry in various shapes

Materials

Templates (edge matched) for equilateral triangles, squares, hexagons and octagons, dotted or squared paper, cubes, plasticine, solid shapes, mirrors, isometric paper, boxes (triangular prism, hexagonal prism, cuboid, cube), everyday objects as suggested in pupils' book

Vocabulary

Axes of symmetry, lines of symmetry, order of rotational symmetry, equilateral triangle, square, hexagon, octagon, quadrilateral, plane of symmetry, centre of rotation, axis of rotation, prism, prediction, diagonal, reflects, reflection, horizontal, vertical

TEACHING POINTS   SECTION A

1 Lines of symmetry

Revise lines of symmetry by looking for shapes in the room that have them. Revise the number of lines of symmetry in regular shapes.

Draw half a shape showing the line of symmetry. Ask the children to complete the shape. This can also be done using squared paper designs.

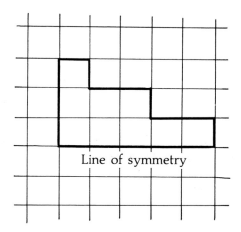

Line of symmetry

2 Curve stitching

It is interesting for children to colour curve stitching patterns and look for lines of symmetry.

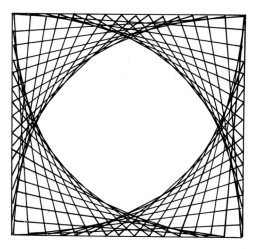

3 Faces

Let the children look at a photograph of a face and discuss its symmetry with them. Use a mirror to show that what sometimes appears to be symmetrical is in fact not completely symmetrical. Let the children place a mirror on the photograph.
What do they find?

4 Rotational symmetry

Ask the children to fold a paper circle into eighths, then make a shape by counting on from any point in ones. What shape do they make? What is its order of rotational symmetry?

Let them try again, counting on in fives and joining points. What is the order of rotational symmetry of this shape?

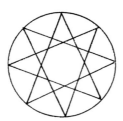

Let the children try counting on using other numbers. Designs of this type can be made on the computer, using Logo.

5 Symmetry patterns

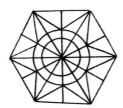

Ask the children to draw round a regular shape template, for example, a hexagon, and to mark all the lines of symmetry. Ask them to draw concentric circles within the shape using the centre point, and then to join other points to make patterns. Let the children investigate the lines of symmetry and rotational symmetry.

6 Planes of symmetry

Revise planes of symmetry with the children. Talk about everyday objects and decide upon their planes of symmetry.

A game to play

FIND THE PLANE

This game is for two small groups.

Each group uses cubes (interlocking or otherwise) and builds a shape which has at least 1 plane of symmetry. They make a note of the number of planes of symmetry it has and then exchange shapes with the other group. They then investigate the planes of symmetry of the other group's shape, write the number, and compare answers.

SECTIONS B AND C

7 Centres of rotation

Look at shapes that have rotational symmetry and talk about the centre of rotation – the point about which a shape rotates and superimposes itself upon itself.

Let the children discuss how they could make a shape with rotational symmetry starting with a strip of squared paper.

 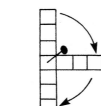 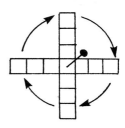

Let them cut other shapes from squared paper and attempt to make new shapes with rotational symmetry.

8 Axes of rotation

Talk with the children about an axis of rotation. You might do this by pushing a thin knitting needle through a Plasticine cuboid and rotating it until it fits on to itself. Discuss how many ways the cuboid would fit on to itself when rotated about this axis, in this case 4.

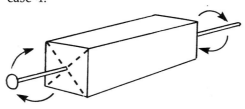

9 Finding planes of symmetry

Revise planes of symmetry with the children. Give out boxes, such
as grocery packages, and let children mark on planes of symmetry
and possibly cut the boxes along the planes. If a suitable sized
mirror is available, this could be used to check the planes.

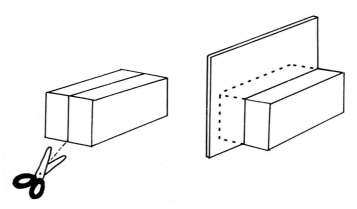

10 Drawing three-dimensional shapes in two dimensions

Discuss how to draw three-dimensional shapes in two dimensions.
Give them isometric paper and let them practise drawing a cube and
a cuboid.

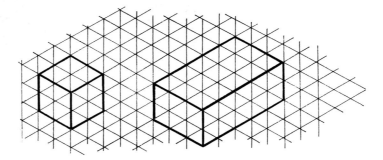

**LINKS WITH THE
ENVIRONMENT**

Talk with the children about symmetry in the environment.

- Look at everyday objects for symmetry.
- Look at symmetry in nature, for example, flower and leaf
  shapes.
- Talk about symmetry in flight and movement, for example,
  birds, bats, aeroplanes, fish, etc.
- Look at applications of rotational symmetry, for example, a
  double-sided car key can be inserted in two positions, logos,
  for example, Isle of Man logo, British Rail sign, etc.
- Look at kaleidoscope patterns.

NOTES ON INVESTIGATIONS

Section A

Do the children appreciate the difference between rotational and line symmetry? Do they devise shapes that have rotational but no line symmetry? For example:

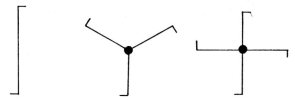

Section B

Do the children appreciate planes of symmetry? Do they devise boxes with appropriate planes of symmetry? For example:

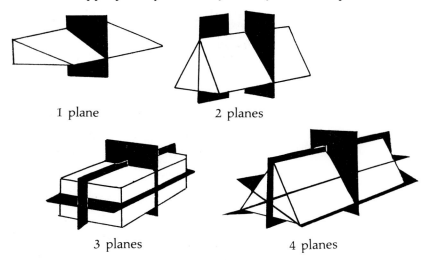

1 plane   2 planes

3 planes   4 planes

Section C

Do the children work systematically through numbers and letters? For example:

0	0
	0

I	I
	I

X	X
	X

H	H
	H

Do the children work through their list of letters to make a word with both horizontal and vertical lines of symmetry? For example:

Number 9

Purpose

- To revise simple number patterns
- To determine possible rules for generating a sequence of numbers
- To introduce square and triangular numbers
- To understand and use terms such as prime, square, cube, square root, cube root, multiples and factors

Materials

Squared paper, hundred square, calculators, dotted paper (in squares)

Vocabulary

Hundred square, corner number, rectangle, odd, even, horizontally, vertically, wall pattern, square numbers, patterns, dot pattern, triples, squared, triangular numbers, cube numbers, cubed, machines, input, output, multiple, multiplying, whole numbers, factors, pairs, multiply together, factor plant, prime numbers, Eratosthenes, Greek astronomer, sieve, sum, results, calculator, square root, answer, difference

TEACHING POINTS   SECTION A

1 Number patterns

Can the children think of any number patterns they see in everyday life? For example, in the page numbers of a book (1, 2, 3, 4, . . .) odd numbers are on right-hand pages and even numbers on left-hand pages. Numbers on houses in a road may give rise to other patterns.

2 Hundred square

Give each child a hundred square or ask them to make one. Divide the children into groups. Ask each group to choose a different number pattern and each child in the group has to colour a different one.

The number patterns are then shown to another group of children who have to describe them in as many ways as possible.

1	2	(3)	4	5	(6)	7	8	(9)	10
11	(12)	13	14	(15)	16	17	(18)	19	20
(21)	22	23	(24)	25	26	(27)	28	29	(30)
31	32	(33)	34	35	(36)	37	38	(39)	40
41	(42)	43	44	(45)	46	47	(48)	49	50
(51)	52	53	(54)	55	56	(57)	58	59	(60)
61	62	(63)	64	65	(66)	67	68	(69)	70
71	(72)	73	74	(75)	76	77	(78)	79	80
(81)	82	83	(84)	85	86	(87)	88	89	(90)
91	92	(93)	94	95	(96)	97	98	(99)	100

counting in 3s
from 3 to 99

1̸	2	3̸	4	5̸	6	7̸	8	9̸	10
1̸1	12	1̸3	14	1̸5	16	1̸7	18	1̸9	20
2̸1	22	2̸3	24	2̸5	26	2̸7	28	2̸9	30
3̸1	32	3̸3	34	3̸5	36	3̸7	38	3̸9	40
4̸1	42	4̸3	44	4̸5	46	4̸7	48	4̸9	50
5̸1	52	5̸3	54	5̸5	56	5̸7	58	5̸9	60
6̸1	62	6̸3	64	6̸5	66	6̸7	68	6̸9	70
7̸1	72	7̸3	74	7̸5	76	7̸7	78	7̸9	80
8̸1	82	8̸3	84	8̸5	86	8̸7	88	8̸9	90
9̸1	92	9̸3	94	9̸5	96	9̸7	98	9̸9	100

odd numbers
from 1 to 99

1	2	(3)	4	5	6	7	8	9	10
11	12	(13)	14	15	16	17	18	19	20
21	22	(23)	24	25	26	27	28	29	30
31	32	(33)	34	35	36	37	38	39	40
41	42	(43)	44	45	46	47	48	49	50
51	52	(53)	54	55	56	57	58	59	60
61	62	(63)	64	65	66	67	68	69	70
71	72	(73)	74	75	76	77	78	79	80
81	82	(83)	84	85	86	87	88	89	90
91	92	(93)	94	95	96	97	98	99	100

counting in 10s
down from 93 to 3

3 Square patterns

Ask the children to mark a 2 by 2 square on their hundred square
grid and add the numbers diagonally. For example:

2	3	15
12	13	15

What do they notice?

What happens if they add the numbers horizontally and vertically?

2	3
12	13

5 ⎫
25 ⎭ 20 difference

14   16
⎵
2 difference

Does this work with any other 2 by 2 square on the grid? Can they explain why?

Ask the children to investigate what happens if the horizontal numbers in a 2 by 2 square are subtracted (difference of 1) and what happens if the vertical numbers are subtracted (difference of 10).

4 Addition square

Ask the children to complete an addition square.

+	0	1	2	3	4	5	6	7	8	9	10
0	0	1	2	3	4	5	6	7	8	9	10
1	1	2	3	4	5	6	7	8	9	10	11
2	2	3	4	5	6	7	8	9	10	11	12
3	3	4	5	6	7	8	9	10	11	12	13
4	4	5	6	7	8	9	10	11	12	13	14
5	5	6	7	8	9	10	11	12	13	14	15
6	6	7	8	9	10	11	12	13	14	15	16
7	7	8	9	10	11	12	13	14	15	16	17
8	8	9	10	11	12	13	14	15	16	17	18
9	9	10	11	12	13	14	15	16	17	18	19
10	10	11	12	13	14	15	16	17	18	19	20

Ask them to talk about any of the patterns they can see. They might suggest the following:

- Horizontally and vertically the numbers increase by 1.
- The diagonals from right to left contain the same number each time.
- The numbers in the diagonals from left to right increase by 2 each time.

Ask the children to choose any 2 by 2 square and investigate the patterns. For example:

3	4
4	5

Let them discuss what happens if you do some of the following:

- add horizontally
- add vertically
- subtract horizontally or vertically
- multiply the diagonals (a calculator may be necessary for this on some squares)

Ask them to investigate whether the results work on other 2 by 2 squares on the addition square.

5 Missing numbers

Write some number patterns on the board and ask children to complete them. For example:

7	8	9	10	□	□	
62	60	58	□	□	52	
3	2	1	□	□	□	−3
10	15	20	□	□	□	40

Ask them to explain how they found the missing numbers.

To reinforce the work in the pupils' book, it might be worth explaining that a 'constant difference' implies a pattern of numbers with the same difference when subtracting. Pattern work involving constant difference and the addition of the previous two numbers in a sequence is developed in the pupils' book.

6 Games to play

FINISH THE PATTERN

Play the game in two teams.

One player from the first team writes four numbers from a number pattern and two missing number boxes. For example:

93   83   73   □   □   43

A player from the second team has to call out the two missing numbers. Only the first numbers called out can be accepted. One point is scored for each correct number called. The teams then change over. The first team to score 25 points is the winner.

Limits may be put on the size of the numbers to suit the ability level of the children, for example, -10 to 10, -100 to 100 or -1000 to 1000. The game could be played using decimals for those children able to cope with this.

FIRST TO 20

Write 'First to 20' and 'add 1 or 2' on the board. Explain that these are the 'rules' and that you will play with a particular child. Ask them to choose who should start (i.e. with number 1 or 2). Play the game with several children, using the number pattern 2, 5, 8, 11, 14, 17, 20 in order to win several games.

Talk about why you keep winning and discuss the number pattern. Ask the children to find the number pattern if the winner was 'First to 21' (i.e. 3, 6, 9, 12, 15, 18, 21) or 'First to 22' (i.e. 1, 4, 7, 10, 13, 16, 19, 22). Discuss whether it is wise to choose to go first.

TAKE

Play the game in pairs.

Each pair of children has 15 counters. Players take turns to remove 1, 2 or 3 counters. The winner is the child who takes the last counter (or counters). For example

15 — 1	Player A takes 1
14 — 3	B takes 3
11 — 2	A takes 2
9 — 1	B takes 1
8 — 3	A takes 3
5 — 1	B takes 1
4 — 2	A takes 2
2 — 2	B takes 2
	B wins

After several games talk about the patterns for winning, i.e. aim to leave 12, 8, 4 counters for an opponent to remove 1, 2 or 3 counters. The game could be played so that the loser is the player who takes the last counter (the winning pattern would be to leave 13, 9, 5, 1 counters).

SECTIONS B AND C

7 The multiplication square

Give the children a multiplication square or let them make one. Ask them to find some number patterns on the square and describe them. For example:

- table patterns
- horizontal and vertical patterns for the same number are the same (this is because of the commutative law)

×	1	2	3	4	5	6	7	8	9	10
1	1	2	3	4	5	6	7	8	9	10
2	2	4	6	8	10	12	14	16	18	20
3	3	6	9	12	15	18	21	24	27	30
4	4	8	12	16	20	24	28	32	36	40
5	5	10	15	20	25	30	35	40	45	50
6	6	12	18	24	30	36	42	48	54	60
7	7	14	21	28	35	42	49	56	63	70
8	8	16	24	32	40	48	56	64	72	80
9	9	18	27	36	45	54	63	72	81	90
10	10	20	30	40	50	60	70	80	90	100

A game to play

FINISH THE PATTERN

Play the game in pairs.

Each player has a multiplication square and a piece of squared paper. Both players draw a different snake pattern on their multiplication square. They copy their snake on to the squared paper, putting in three numbers in the correct positions. They then exchange their pieces of squared paper and try to complete the opponent's snake pattern without looking at a multiplication square. The first player to complete it correctly is the winner.

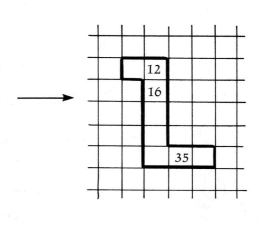

8 Square numbers

Ask the children to use the multiplication square and colour the answers to numbers which are multiplied by themselves: 1×1, 2×2, 3×3, 4×4, etc. What do they notice? (The numbers lie on the diagonal from top left to bottom right.) Explain that these are the square numbers and can be built up from squares on the multiplication square.

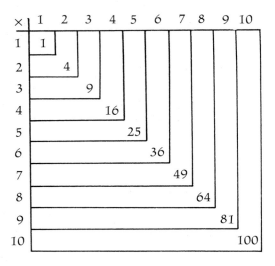

Talk about recording square numbers as

$$1 \times 1 \qquad 2 \times 2 \qquad 3 \times 3 \ldots$$

and

$$1^2 \qquad 2^2 \qquad 3^2 \quad \ldots$$

Can they work out 5^2, 9^2, etc.?
   Square numbers are developed in the pupils' book.

9 Investigating square patterns

Ask the children to mark a 2 by 2 square on their multiplication square. Ask them to find what happens if they do the following:

- subtract the numbers horizontally
- subtract the numbers vertically
- multiply the diagonals
- add the diagonals and find the difference.

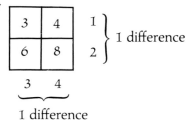

Ask the children to do similar investigations on 3 by 3 squares, 4 by 4 squares, etc. Can they describe and explain their findings?

10 Triangular numbers

Explain to the children that a triangle can be drawn around particular numbers of similar counters or similar balls. For example:

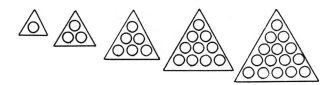

Ask them where they may have seen triangle patterns like this in everyday life (snooker). The number pattern of counters (or balls) form the triangular number pattern 1, 3, 6, 10, 15, . . . Ask them to describe the pattern and to work out the first and second differences:

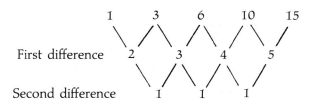

Triangular numbers are developed in the pupils' book.

Ask the children to draw an arrangement of cans to knock off the shelf at a fairground:

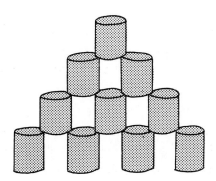

Can they recognise the triangular number pattern in each row of the cans?

11 Cube numbers

Cube numbers are introduced in the pupils' book by making larger cubes from smaller ones and introducing a method of recording.

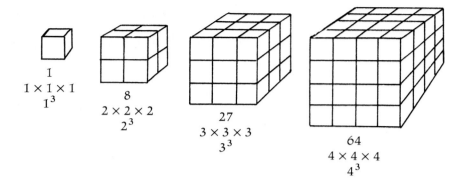

It might be necessary to have a number of small cubes for the children to do this practically and so build up the mental imagery. Ask the children to explain how we can record $5 \times 5 \times 5$ as 5^3 and $6^3 = \square \times \square \times \square$. Can they work out the answer?

12 Factors

Talk with the children about factors. Ask them to find the factors of 10, that is, pairs of numbers that multiply together to make 10 $(1 \times 10, 2 \times 5)$.

Remind them how to find factors of any number on the multiplication square. Let them choose a number and follow the horizontal and vertical line from that number to find its factors. Explain that 1 and the number itself are also factors. Ask them to find all the factors of 18 $(1 \times 18, 2 \times 9, 3 \times 6)$. Explain that these can be arranged as follows:

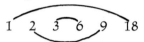

Explain that factors can be shown in interesting ways. For example:

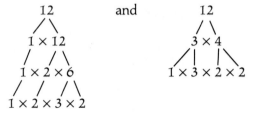

Ask them to show other numbers in a similar way.

The work on factors is developed in the pupils' book.

13 Prime numbers

Talk about prime numbers. Explain that a prime number has exactly one pair of factors, 1 and the number itself. Point out that 1 is not a prime number because it does not have two different factors.

Ask the children to find prime numbers between 12 and 20 (13, 17, 19). Can they find any between 20 and 30?

The work on prime numbers is developed in the pupils' book.

14 Multiples

Talk with the children about multiples. Explain that multiples of 5 are found by multiplying 5 by whole numbers:

5, 10, 15, 20, 25, 30, . . .

Give the children a multiplication square and ask them to colour all the multiples of 3. Then let them colour the multiples of 4. What do they notice about numbers like *12, 24, 36*? (They are common multiples.) Are 3 and 4 both factors of these numbers?

Ask them to find multiples that are in both the 2s and 5s pattern.

Work on multiples is extended in the pupils book.

15 Number grids

Draw a grid on the board. Explain that numbers written on the grid are multiplied by the number shown and in the direction of the arrows:

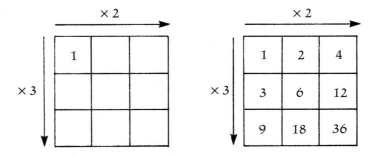

Point out that numbers in the positions by 6, 12, 18, 36 (in this case) in the completed grid are multiples of 2 and 3. Ask the children to complete other grids in a similar way.

Can the children complete the grids when some of the numbers are missing? For example:

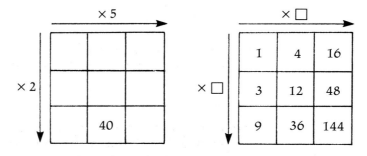

A game to play

GRIDS

This game is for two teams.

A player from the first team draws a 3 by 3 grid and completes part of it as in the previous activity. A player from the second team has to fill in the missing numbers correctly to complete the grid and score 1 point. The teams then change over. The team that scores the most points wins.

MENTAL WORK   Ask the children appropriate mental questions involving the following:

- Number patterns – Find the missing numbers in the following patterns:

    2   4   6   8   ☐   ☐
    1000   900   800   700   ☐   ☐
    7   5   3   1   ☐   ☐

- Multiplication tables, for example $9 \times 8 = \square$, $7 \times 5 = \square$
- Square numbers – What is 4 squared? What is the seventh square number? What is 1 squared plus 2 squared?
- Triangular numbers – What is the third number in the triangular number pattern?
- Factors – What are the factors of 12? How many factors has 9?
- Multiples – Of which numbers is 15 a multiple?
- Prime numbers – Which prime number is between 8 and 12?

A game to play

FIND THE NUMBER

Write the following statements on the board:

factor of	multiple of
square number	prime number
greater than	less than
triangular number	

Explain to the children that you are thinking of a number between 1 and 20. They have to find the number by asking questions using the statements above. For example, is it a multiple of 5?
Point out that you can only answer 'yes' or 'no'.

This could be made into a game for groups of children to play, drawing a card from a set of number cards.

USING THE CALCULATOR

- Use the constant function to make number patterns including negative numbers, square numbers and multiples.
- Introduce the square root key (section C only). Ask the children to find the square root of some of the square numbers. For example 25, 49. Ask them what happens if you multiply the answer by itself. (The work on square roots is developed in section C of the pupils' book.)
- Ask the children to find the cube of 2.

$$2^3 = 2 \times 2 \times 2 = 8$$

Point out that the cube root of 8 is 2.

$$\sqrt[3]{8} = 2.$$

Ask them to find the cube root of the following numbers: 27, 64, 1000.

LINKS WITH THE ENVIRONMENT

Talk about everyday situations involving number patterns.

- At school – hundred square, addition square, multiplication square, page numbers in a book, left-hand pages, right-hand pages, crayons and felt tips often come in packets of 8, the calculator is used for number patterns and finding square roots.
- In the street – house numbers, bus numbers (are any numbers multiples of 2, 5, 10?).
- At the fairground or circus – cans balanced on a shelf to knock off in three tries, acrobats, trick motor-cyclists may form a human pyramid (triangular numbers).
- At the supermarket – tins are often arranged in triangular numbers.
- Sport – snooker balls are arranged in triangular numbers.

NOTES ON INVESTIGATIONS

Section A

Do the children complete the number pattern in a logical manner? Do they appreciate that there are many ways to do it?

Section B

Do the children find different prime numbers which are the sum of two square numbers? For example:

$$1 + 4 = 5 \qquad 16 + 25 = 41$$
$$4 + 9 = 13 \qquad 4 + 49 = 53$$
$$4 + 25 = 29 \qquad 9 + 64 = 73$$
$$1 + 36 = 37 \qquad 16 + 81 = 97$$

Section C

Do the children devise a system to find the chosen number?
Do they use all the different patterns and mathematical ideas (i.e. multiples, factors, prime numbers, triangular number patterns)?
Do they conclude that the missing number is 12?
Do they use a variety of different number patterns in making up their own problems?

Time and shape

Purpose

- To revise 24-hour clock times
- To introduce time zones
- To use networks
- To introduce nodes, arcs and regions

Materials

Atlases or a globe, a 24-hour clock, paper for drawing network diagrams

Vocabulary

Earth, rotate, sun rises, divided, time zones, Greenwich, standard time, east, ahead, west, behind, local time, node, arc, region, network diagram

TEACHING POINTS   SECTION A

1 24-hour clock times

Talk with the children about 24-hour clock times and where they might see them, for example, in railway timetables. Do they

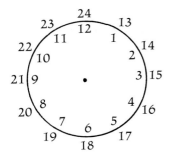

remember how to work them out? For example:

> 5 p.m. is 5 hours after midday or 12:00
> so it is 12:00 + 5 hours → 17:00

Draw a 24-hour clock face on the board to remind them of the times. Give them practice in converting 'o'clock' times to 24-hour clock times. Remind them that 24-hour clock times are always written as four-digit numbers:

> 8 a.m. → 08:00

Remind them also that we do not need to write a.m. or p.m. when using 24-hour clock times.

A game to play

MATCH THE TIME

This game is for two groups.
    Make flash cards for pairs of matching times, 'o'clock' and 24-hour clock

| 6 p.m. | 18:00 | 7 a.m. | 07:00 |

Duplicate them and give an identical set to each of the groups. The cards are shuffled. At a given signal the groups have to match the cards in pairs. The first group to match all the cards correctly is the winner.

2 Time zones

Talk with the children about how the world is a sphere which rotates once every 24 hours. It therefore takes 24 hours for the world to rotate through an angle of 360°. This means that the sun rises in different places at different times. Places to the east of us have sun-rise before us and therefore are ahead of us in time whilst places to the west of us have sun-rise after us and are therefore behind us in time. Do the children see the effects this has on times around the world?
    Ask the children to use their calculators to find out how many degrees the Earth rotates through in 1 hour: 360° ÷ 24 = 15° in one hour. Explain how the world is divided into one-hour time zones and that each zone is between two lines running north to south on a map or globe at 15° intervals. Time zones were adopted in 1883. Look at these lines on a map or globe.
    Do the children notice that large countries have a number of them and therefore a number of time zones? Talk about the practicalities of this and how sometimes time zones are adjusted to suit boundaries.

3 Standard time

Do the children notice that longitude 0° passes through London (Greenwich to be exact)? Talk about how the time in Greenwich is taken as the Standard Time. Countries to the east of Greenwich, London, are ahead in time and countries to the west are behind in time.

4 Time around the world

Ask the children to look in their atlases to find cities that are ahead of London in time and some that are behind it. Have any of them ever travelled to a country that is in a different time zone? Did they have to adjust their watch? Has anyone had to do this whilst travelling on a plane?

Sydney, Australia, is 10 hours ahead of us in time. Ask questions about the time difference.

> What line of longitude is Sydney on?
> How many away from 0° is this?
> What will the time in Sydney be now?
> What will be children there probably be doing?
> What time will it be here as they are starting morning school there?

For details of times around the world, encourage the children to look for information in atlases, geography textbooks, reference books and, possibly, travel agents.

5 Recording time zones

Explain that in the pupils' book the time zones are shown in two ways:
Places ahead of Greenwich, London, in time are shown as + hours.
Places behind Greenwich in time are shown as − hours.
For example, Athens is + 2 hours and New York is − 5 hours.

A game to play

BEFORE AND AFTER

This game is for two groups.

Give each group an identical set of flash cards of well-known cities around the world. The groups have to sort the cities into those ahead of Greenwich in time and those behind it. For example:

	0°
− hours	+ hours
Los Angeles	Perth

The first group to do so correctly is the winner.

SECTIONS B AND C

6 Network diagrams

Talk with the children about network diagrams and how they can be plans which show how places are linked. Draw a simple network diagram of the local area. For example:

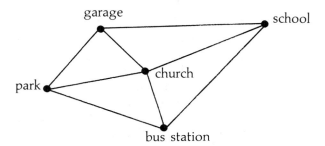

Discuss possible routes from the park to the school.

Explain nodes, arcs and regions. In the diagram each road is an arc and the nodes are the points where the roads meet. The regions are the areas separated by the arcs. Draw the network again to illustrate this:

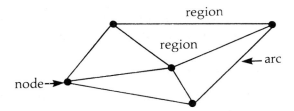

Ask the children to count the number of nodes, regions and arcs in the network diagram: 5 nodes, 8 arcs and 5 regions (point out that the 'outer' area is also a region).

7 Traversability

Draw network diagrams and ask the children if they can travel along every road or arc without retracing their path along any road. Explain that they can show this by attempting to draw the network without taking their pencil from the paper or going over any line twice. Networks are said to be traversable if this can be done.

The pupils' book leads the children to discover that a network is only traversable if none of the nodes or only two of the nodes have an odd number of arcs leading into them. Traversability is not affected by nodes which have an even number of arcs leading into them. For example:

Traversable – 2 nodes have an odd number of arcs leading into them

Traversable – 0 nodes with an odd number of arcs leading into them

Not traversable – 4 nodes with an odd number of arcs leading into them.

A puzzle to try

Ask the children to draw this shape without lifting their pencil from the paper and without going over the same line twice.

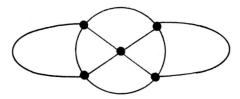

MENTAL WORK

- Give the children practice in converting 12-hour to 24-hour times and vice versa. For example:

  2 p.m. → ☐ ☐ : ☐ ☐
  17:00 → ☐ a.m. or p.m.

- Give practice in adding and subtracting times. Ask verbal questions such as: 'It is now 3 o'clock. What time will it be 6 hours from now? What time was it 6 hours ago?'

LINKS WITH THE ENVIRONMENT

Talk with the children about time zones.

- How many of them have travelled to a place in another time zone? Did they have to adjust their watches? By how much?
- How many of them have made phone calls to relatives or friends in another part of the world and have had to decide on the best time to make the call?
- Talk about people who travel as part of their job, such as airline pilots, and are constantly changing time zones.
- Talk about news coverage of events around the world. For example, when cricket test matches or the Olympic Games are being held in different time zones to our own (e.g. Los Angeles —8 hours).

Talk about such network diagrams as the London Underground tube map.

NOTES ON INVESTIGATIONS

Section A

Do the children consider the time zones when working out their phone calls to other cities, taking London (Greenwich) as a reference point? Do they take 12:00 local time and then add or subtract the difference in hours?

Section B

Do the children draw appropriate network diagrams and remember to count the 'outside' region? Do they discover the relationship $N+R=A+2$?

Section C

This is the famous Koenigsberg Bridge problem solved by the mathematician Euler in 1737. The network for the seven bridges is:

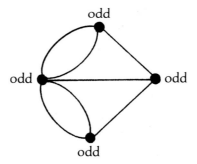

This is not traversable as it has four odd nodes. If another bridge is added the network becomes:

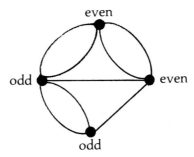

This is traversable as it now has only two odd nodes.

Module 7 Pupils' book 1
RECORD SHEET ▮▮▮▮▮▮▮▮▮▮▮

Class. . . . . Pupil . . . .

Topic	Section	Assessment	Comment
Money 1	A B C		
Shape 1	A B C		
Number 1	A B C		
Length	A B C		
Area	A B C		
Volume	A B C		
Probability 1	A B C		
Map reading	A B C		
Data 1	A B C		
Percentages	A B C		

General comments:

Module 7 Pupils' book 2
RECORD SHEET ▬▬▬▬▬▬▬▬▬

Class . . . .   Pupil . . . .

Topic	Section			Assessment	Comment
Number 2	A	B	C		
Number 3	A	B	C		
Data 2	A	B	C		
Probability 2	A	B	C		
Angles 1	A	B	C		
Measurement 1	A	B	C		
Number 4	A	B	C		
Co-ordinates	A	B	C		
Data 3	A	B	C		
Number 5	A	B	C		
Number 6	A	B	C		
Angles 2	A	B	C		
Number 7	A	B	C		
Measurement 2	A	B	C		
Number 8	A	B	C		
Shape 2	A	B	C		
Number 9	A	B	C		
Time and shape	A	B	C		

General comments:

MATERIALS REQUIRED FOR MODULE 7 ▬▬▬▬▬

24-hour clock
angle measurers
atlas
baked beans tin
bathroom scales
blank hundred squares
boxes (triangular prism,
    hexagonal prism, cuboid,
    cube)
calculators
capacity jugs or measurers
car brochures and magazines
card
centimetre cubes
centimetre squared paper
circular protractors
clinometer
clock stamp
comics
computer (if available)
counters
counters with O on one side
    and X on the other
cubes (yellow and blue)
dice
dotted paper (cm²)
educational supplier's
    catalogue
geo-boards
glue
height measure

Highway Code
isometric paper
large squared paper
long tape measure
magazines
maps (various kinds,
    including Ordnance
    Survey)
metre stick
mirrors
newspapers showing
    exchange rates for different
    currencies and world
    temperatures
objects for weighing
orange
packs of playing cards
paper
paper labels
plain paper
plans of the school, houses,
    safari parks etc.
Plasticine
pots
protractors
reels (red, blue and yellow)
reference books (about
    animals, Europe, famous
    buildings, geography,
    sport)
rulers

scissors
small bags (not transparent)
soap powder boxes (E3 and
    other sizes)
solid shapes
squared paper
stationery catalogue
stop watch
strong paper
tape measures
templates (equilateral
    triangle, square, regular
    hexagon, regular octagon
    – the edges of which are
    all the same length;
    different quadrilaterals)
thermometer
tie
timer
tracing paper
various jugs and containers
watch or timer with a second
    hand
weighing scales
world globe

GLOSSARY FOR MODULE 7

acute angle	An angle between 0° and 90°.
alternate angles	The pair of equal angles that are formed when a line crosses a pair of parallel lines.

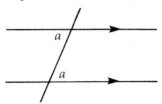

angle	An angle is the amount of turn or rotation. Angles are measured in degrees with 360° in a whole turn.
angle measurer	*See* protractor.
angle of elevation	The angle measured up from the horizontal to the top of an object.

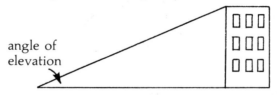

anti-clockwise	*See* clockwise.
approximate	A number or measurement which is not exact but is accepted as being close enough.
arc	An arc joins two nodes in a network.

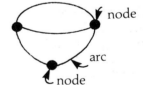

area	Area is the size or amount of a surface, and is usually written in units of square measurement.
average (mean)	The mean of a set of numbers is the sum of the numbers divided by the number of them in the set. For example, the mean of 1, 4, 5 and 6 is

$$\frac{1+4+5+6}{4} = \frac{16}{4} = 4$$

axis (pl. axes)	One of the reference lines on a graph.

axis of rotation   A line about which an object can rotate to fit onto itself.

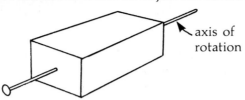

bar chart   A form of pictorial representation where the data is represented by bars or columns.

bar-line graph   A form of graph where the data is represented by lines.

bearing   The clockwise angle between the north line and the line to an object. It is given as three digits.

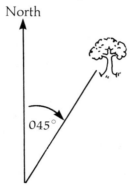

bilateral symmetry   *See* line symmetry.

block graph   A block graph is a form of pictorial representation where the data is represented by columns.

capacity   The capacity of a container is the amount that it will hold.

Celsius   A temperature scale where 0 °C is the freezing point of water and 100 °C is the boiling point.

Centigrade   A temperature scale where 0 °C is the freezing point of water and 100 °C is the boiling point. It is now known as the Celsius scale.

centimetre $\frac{1}{100}$ of a metre (abbreviation: cm).

chain   An Imperial unit of length equal to 22 yards.

centre of rotation   The point that remains fixed when a shape is rotated.

circumference   The circumference is the distance around a circle.

class intervals   Data is sometimes grouped into classes (usually equal) to give a clearer idea of the distribution.
For example, marks of 1–50 may be grouped as 1–10, 11–20, etc.

clinometer	An instrument for measuring angles of elevation.
clockwise	This is the direction in which the hands of a clock turn. Anti-clockwise is the opposite direction.
commutative	An operation, for example $+$, $-$, is commutative if numbers can be used with it in any order and still give the same answer. Addition is commutative, since, for example, $3 + 1 = 1 + 3$. Multiplication is commutative, since, for example, $3 \times 2 = 2 \times 3$. Subtraction is **not** commutative, since $3 - 1 \neq 1 - 3$. Division is **not** commutative, since $4 \div 2 \neq 2 \div 4$.
compass	An instrument for showing direction. The four points of the compass are N, S, E, W. The eight points of the compass are N, S, E, W, NW, NE, SE, SW.
complementary angles	If two angles, e.g. 40° and 50°, add up to 90°, they are complementary.
congruent	Figures are congruent if they are identical in shape and size.
concentric circles	Circles with the same centre.
constant function	The use of the constant function on a calculator allows numbers to increase or decrease by a fixed amount. For example, the numbers 2, 5, 8, 11, . . . are increasing by the constant $+3$.
continuous	Without a break in values. For example, length is a continuous quantity because it may be any intermediate value between, for example, 1 cm and 2 cm (it does not have to be one or the other). If a quantity is not continuous it is said to be discrete. Discrete, or separate, quantities can be counted.
co-ordinates	An ordered pair of numbers, for example (4, 5), to show a point on a graph or gird.

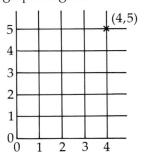

corresponding angles	If a line crosses a pair of parallel lines, the angles in corresponding positions will be equal

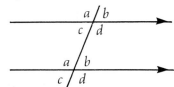

cube	A cube is a solid with all its six faces square and all its edges equal in length. For example, a die is a cube.

cube number	The third power of the number. For example 2 'cubed' is $2 \times 2 \times 2 = 2^3 = 8$.
cube root	$3 \times 3 \times 3 = 27$ so 3 is the cube root of 27. Similarly, 2 is the cube root of 8.
cubic centimetre	A unit of volume (abbreviation: cm³).
cuboid	A cuboid is a solid with six faces that are all rectangles. Opposite faces are the same.
cylinder	A cylinder is a solid with the shape of a circle along its length.
data	Data is information or facts which have been collected. It is often displayed as a block graph or bar chart.
database	A collection of organised information or data.
decimal fraction	A fraction with a denominator of 10, 100, 1000 etc. which is written using a decimal point.
decimal notation	A way of writing numbers that involves a decimal point. For example, a length of 5 metres 23 centimetres can be written in decimal notation as 5·23 m.
decimal places	The number of digits after the decimal point.
decimal point	A point placed after the units digit and before the tenths, hundredths, etc.
decision tree diagram	A diagram, often used to sort objects into sets, with boxes where questions are asked. The answer Yes or No determines which of two paths to take to the next box.
degree (temperature)	A degree is a temperature interval. The most common scales are Celsius and Fahrenheit.
degrees	Angles are measured in degrees. There are $360°$ in a full turn.
denominator	The bottom part of a fraction. It shows how many equal parts the quantity has been split into.
diagonal	A diagonal is a straight line drawn from one vertex of a shape to another non-adjacent vertex. For example

diagonal

diagonals

diameter	A diameter is any straight line that joins two points of a circle and passes through the centre.
digit	A digit is a single figure or symbol in a number system. For example, the digits in 347 are 3, 4 and 7.
discrete	*See* continuous.

eastings	The numbers increasing from west to east on a map grid.
edge	An edge is the line formed when two faces of a solid meet.

equal chance	An equal chance is when every possible outcome has the same chance of happening. For example, there is an equal chance of throwing 1, 2, 3, 4, 5 or 6 on a fair die.
equilateral triangle	An equilateral triangle is a triangle with all three sides the same length.
equivalent fractions	Fractions are equivalent if they can represent the same fraction. For example, $\frac{1}{2}, \frac{2}{4}, \frac{3}{6}, \frac{4}{8}, \frac{5}{10}, \frac{6}{12}$ are equivalent.
estimate	To estimate is to make an approximate judgement of a number, amount, etc. without measuring it.
even chance	A one in two chance or 50/50 chance of happening.
even number	A whole number which is exactly divisible by 2.
face	A face is the flat side of a solid shape.
factor	A factor is a number which divides exactly into another number. For example, 3 is a factor of 12.
Fahrenheit	A temperature scale where $32\,^\circ$F is the freezing point of water and $212\,^\circ$F is the boiling point.
fair chance	*See* equal chance.
foot (ft)	An Imperial unit of length. 1 foot $=$ 12 inches. 3 feet $=$ 1 yard.
formula	An equation that shows the relationship between quantities. For example, the formula for the perimeter of a square of side l is $P = 4l$.
fraction	A number less than 1, written as $\frac{a}{b}$ where a is the numerator and b is the denominator.
freezing point	The temperature at which a liquid freezes.
frequency chart	A bar chart showing frequency on one of its axes.
function machine	A machine that operates on numbers. For example,

$$\text{INPUT} \xrightarrow{2} \boxed{\overset{\text{machine}}{+3}} \rightarrow 5 \ \text{OUTPUT}$$

furlong	An Imperial unit of length. 8 furlongs $=$ 1 mile.
gallon	An Imperial unit of capacity equal to 8 pints.
gram	A gram is a unit of weight. It is $\frac{1}{1000}$ of a kilogram. The abbreviation for gram is g.
grid	A set of intersecting parallel lines, usually at right angles to one another and the same distance apart.
grouped data	Data which has been grouped together. For example, marks may be grouped into classes of 0–9, 10–19, 20–29, etc.

hexagon	A hexagon is a plane shape with six sides. A regular hexagon has all its sides equal in length and all its angles the same size.
hexagonal prism	A prism with end faces that are hexagons.
horizontal	A line is horizontal when it is parallel to the Earth's horizon. It is at right angles to a vertical line.
horizontal axis	A graph usually has two axes, the horizontal (x axis) and the vertical (y axis).

vertical
axis

horizontal
axis

hundredweight (cwt)	An Imperial unit of weight. 1 cwt = 112 lb. 20 cwt = 1 ton.
Imperial units	Units of measurement still used, in part, in the UK but now giving way to metric units. Examples of Imperial units include yards, stones and gallons.
inch	An Imperial unit of length. 12 inches = 1 foot.
intersecting lines	Lines that cross or meet.
irregular shape	A shape that is not regular. All of its sides and angles are not equal.
isometric paper	Paper with a grid of equilateral triangles.
isosceles triangle	A triangle with two equal sides.
kilogram (kg)	The standard unit of weight equal to 1000 grams.
kilometre (km)	A metric unit of length equal to 1000 metres.
kite	A quadrilateral that has two pairs of equal and adjacent sides.
leap year	A year with 366 days.
line graph	A graph that shows data by means of a line.
line of symmetry	A line of symmetry on a plane shape divides the shape so that one half is a mirror image of the other.
line symmetry	The exact matching of parts on either side of a straight line. This is sometimes called bilateral, mirror, or reflective symmetry.
litre	A litre is a unit of capacity (abbreviation: l, not to be confused with 1). One litre is a little over $1\frac{3}{4}$ pints.
Logo	A computer language which allows control of a 'turtle' on the screen.
maximum	The highest value.
mean	*See* average.
metre (m)	A metre is the standard unit of length. 1000 m = 1 km

metric	A system of units based on the metre, litre and kilogram and using multiples of 10.
mile	An Imperial unit of length equal to 1760 yards.
millilitre (ml)	$\frac{1}{1000}$ of a litre.
million	A million is a thousand thousand.
minimum	The lowest value.
minute	A minute is 60 seconds.
multiple	Multiples of a number are given by that number multiplied by whole numbers. The multiples of 4 are 4, 8, 12, 16, . . . The multiples of 10 are 10, 20, 30, 40, . . .
negative number	A number less than zero. For example, -1 is one less than zero.
net	A two-dimensional shape that can be folded to make a three-dimensional shape. For example, is a net for a
network	A network is a diagram of connected lines. The lines of the diagram are called arcs. The points where the arcs meet are called nodes. The areas for which the lines form a boundary are called regions. 5 nodes 8 arcs 5 regions
node	A node is the point at the beginning and end of every arc on a network diagram. For example 3 nodes
northings	The numbers increasing from south to north on a map grid.
numerator	The top part of a fraction. It shows how many of the equal parts are needed.
obtuse angle	An angle between 90° and 180°.
octagon	An eight-sided closed plane shape.
odd number	A whole number not exactly divisible by 2.
order of rotation	The number of times a shape or object fits exactly onto its outline during one full turn. order of rotation 4
ounce (oz)	An Imperial unit of weight. 16 oz = 1 lb.
palindrome	A number or word that reads the same forwards as backwards. For example 999 or 525 or did.

parallel   A set of lines are parallel if they never meet.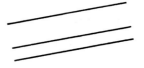

parallelogram   A four-sided shape with opposite sides equal and parallel.

pentagon   A pentagon is a five-sided closed shape. A regular pentagon has all its sides equal in length and all its angles the same size.

percentage   The number of hundredths. For example 30% or 30 per cent is $\frac{30}{100}$.

perimeter   The distance all the way round a closed shape.

perpendicular   Perpendicular lines cross at right angles. For example

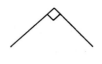

pie chart   A circular diagram divided to represent data, e.g.

6 women
2 men
4 boys
4 girls

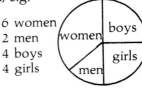

pint (pt)   An Imperial unit of capacity. 8 pints = 1 gallon.

plane of symmetry   A three-dimensional shape may possess a plane of symmetry where one half of the shape is a reflection of the other. For example

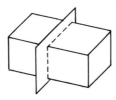

plane shape   A plane shape is a two-dimensional shape. For example, circles and triangles are plane shapes.

plane symmetry   The exact matching of parts on either side of a plane. This is sometimes called mirror or reflective symmetry.

pound (lb)   An Imperial unit of weight. 16 oz = 1 lb. A pound is slightly less than $\frac{1}{2}$ kg.

prime number   A prime number has only one pair of factors 1 and the number itself.

prism   A prism is a solid with the same shape along its length, so that it has uniform cross-section. Prisms take their name from the end face.

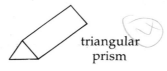
triangular prism

hexagonal prism

probability Probability is the likelihood of an event happening.

probability scale A scale for scoring the likelihood of an event happening.

profit Profit is revenue minus expenditure.

protractor An instrument for measuring angles.
An angle measurer.

pyramid A pyramid is a solid shape with a polygon for its base. The other faces are triangles which meet at a vertex called the apex.

apex

quadrant A fourth part. When drawing a graph the first quadrant is as shown:

first quadrant

quadrilateral A quadrilateral is a four-sided closed plane shape. For example squares, rectangles, trapeziums, rhombuses are all quadrilaterals.

quart An Imperial unit of capacity equal to 2 pints. There are 4 quarts in a gallon.

quire A quire is 24 sheets of paper.

random A random number is a number made or generated by chance and not in a pattern.

range The range of a set of data is the difference between the greatest and the smallest value in the set.

ream A ream is 480 sheets of paper or 20 quires. It is often 500 sheets to allow for wastage.

rectangle A rectangle is a four-sided closed plane shape with four right-angles and opposite sides equal in length.

reflective symmetry *See* line symmetry, plane symmetry.

reflex angle An angle greater than $180°$ but less than $360°$.

region In a network diagram a region is a space bounded by arcs. For example, this network diagram has 2 regions.

region   region

regular shape A regular shape has all its sides the same length and all its angles the same size, for example, a square.

rhombus A quadrilateral with four equal sides.

right-angle A right-angle is a quarter of a complete turn. It is measured as an angle of $90°$.

rotational symmetry   The symmetry of a shape or object fitting exactly into its outline while it rotates about a point or line.

rounding   Writing a number to a required level of accuracy. 126 is written as 130 when rounded (up) to the nearest 10. 124 is written as 120 when rounded (down) to the nearest 10.

scale   The ratio between the size of a model, drawing or map and the size of the object it represents.

scalene triangle   A scalene triangle is a triangle whose sides are all different lengths. N.B. A scalene triangle can have a right angle.

scatter graph   A scatter graph is a way of representing data consisting of pairs of values.

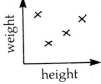

set square   A set square is a measuring instrument containing a right angle. For example

significant figures   The most significant figure or digit in a number is the first digit (not zero) when reading from left to right. For example
2186: 2 is the most significant figure.
2186 becomes 2000 rounded to one significant figure.
2186 becomes 2200 rounded to two significant figures.
0·072 becomes 0·07 rounded to one significant figure.

sphere   A sphere is the mathematical name for a solid round ball.

square   A square has four equal sides and four right-angles.

square centimetre   A unit of area (abbreviation: cm²).

square number   The result of multiplying a whole number by itself.

square root $3 \times 3 = 9$ so 3 is the square root of 9. Similarly, 2 is the square root of 4.

stone   An Imperial unit of weight. $14\,\text{lb} = 1$ stone.

straight angle $180°$.

straight line graph   A graph which is a straight line.

stride   A stride is a long step measured by the distance from heel to heel or toe to toe.

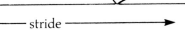
stride

supplementary angles   Two angles which add up to 180° are supplementary. For example, 110° and 70°.

structural apparatus   Structural apparatus is apparatus to show how the number system works.

symmetry   *See* line symmetry, plane symmetry, rotational symmetry.

temperature   A measure of hotness or coldness.

temperature range   The temperature range is the difference between the highest and lowest temperature.

tessellate   A shape or shapes repeat to form a pattern without gaps or overlaps.

tetrahedron   A solid shape with four triangular faces.

time zone   The world is divided into 24 time zones, each between two lines running north to south approximately at 15° intervals. The time is uniform throughout each zone, and each is one hour behind the zone to the east of it. The time at Greenwich is taken as the Standard Time.

ton   An Imperial measure of weight equal to 2240 lb.

tonne   A metric unit of weight. It is 1000 kilograms.

total   The total is the sum which numbers add up to. For example 4 + 5 + 7 = 16; 16 is the total.

trapezium   A quadrilateral with one pair of parallel sides.

traversability   A network is traversable if it can be drawn without going over the same line twice or taking a pencil off the paper. This shape is traversable.

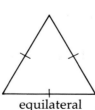 This is not

triangle   A triangle is a closed plane shape with three straight sides.

equilateral   isosceles   right-angled   scalene

triangular number   A triangular number is part of the number pattern 1, 3, 6, 10, 15, 21, . . .

It can be shown as a pattern of dots in the shape of a triangle. For example

triangular prism   A triangular prism is a prism whose end faces are triangles.

two-way table   A two-way table is a way of representing data. For example

	fish	chips	peas
John	✓	✓	✓
Peter	✓		✓
Andrew		✓	✓

unitary ratio   A unitary ratio is often used in scale drawing. For example $1:2$, $1:10$, $1:100$.

vertex (*plural* vertices) The vertex is a point where lines or edges meet.

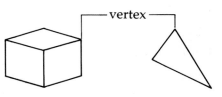

vertical   At right angles to the horizontal.

vertical axis   *See* horizontal axis.

vertically opposite angles Vertically opposite angles are equal.

vertices   *See* vertex.

volume   The volume of a solid is the amount of space it occupies. The units of measurement are usually cubic centimetres or cubic metres.

weight   The weight of an object depends on the gravitational force acting on it. An object on the Moon will weigh less than on Earth although its mass will remain the same.

yard (yd)   An Imperial unit of length. 36 inches = 1 yd, 3 ft = 1 yd.